Learning in Safe Schools

Creating classrooms where all students belong

2nd edition

FAYE BROWNLIE

JUDITH KING

Pembroke Publishers Limited

This book is dedicated to our mothers:
Lillian Brownlie and Helen King,
who taught us all about the journey.

© 2011 Pembroke Publishers
538 Hood Road
Markham, Ontario, Canada L3R 3K9
www.pembrokepublishers.com

Distributed in the U.S. by Stenhouse Publishers
480 Congress Street
Portland, ME 04101
www.stenhouse.com

We acknowledge the financial support of the Government of Canada through the Book Publishing Industry Development Program (BPIDP) for our publishing activities.

We acknowledge the assistance of the Government of Ontario through the Ontario Media Development Corporation's Ontario Book Initiative.

Library and Archives Canada Cataloguing in Publication

Brownlie, Faye
    Learning in safe schools / Faye Brownlie & Judith King. -- 2nd ed.

Includes bibliographical references and index.
Issued also in electronic format.
ISBN 978-1-55138-266-1

    1. Inclusive education. 2. Classroom environment. 3. Curriculum planning.
I. King, Judith, 1954- II. Title.

LC1200.B757 2011   371.9'046   C2011-904793-4

eBook format ISBN 978-1-55138-831-1

Editor: Kat Mototsune
Cover Design: John Zehethofer
Typesetting: Jay Tee Graphics Ltd.

Printed and bound in Canada
9 8 7 6 5 4 3 2 1

Contents

Preface to the Second Edition

In the ten years since the publication of *Learning in Safe Schools*, we have been humbled and honored by the educators we have met who have been influenced by the ideas we presented — building school-wide codes of conduct, focusing explicitly on belonging in the classroom, working with class reviews, changing models of service delivery to support students with special needs, designing lessons with adaptations and modifications, working with learning journeys. Our classrooms and our schools have continued to grow in their diversity. We continue to embrace the challenge of how best to meet the ever-changing needs of education and make all classrooms and schools safe places for all learners, places where all can be the best they can be.

In this edition, we have kept what educators have told us has most made a difference in their schools: chapters 1 to 3 and 11 (chapter 9 in the first edition). We have expanded many chapters — chapters 4, 8, 9, and 10; (chapters 5 to 8 in the first edition) — to include more middle- and secondary-school examples and to address the new realities: shrinking budgets, increased numbers of students learning English, increased numbers of students diagnosed with autism, increased numbers of First Nations learners, a focus on personalized learning. We have drawn from our experiences and from the experiences of educators who have expanded and personalized our ideas.

We believe that inclusion is much more than just being there. It is a general education principle, not a special education initiative. We believe that all students need a safe environment. They need to belong and they need to achieve as learners. With this in mind, we have expanded the focus on learning and included three new chapters (chapters 5, 6, and 7) that specifically address structures and strategies that teachers can use with their classes to build safe environments that support and challenge all learners, acknowledging their strengths and unique talents.

Enjoy this second edition! We invite you to continue to work with your colleagues to build an inclusive school, teach so all can learn, and take ownership of all students.

Introduction: Inclusion as We See It

There has been a move in the educational community over the past twenty years to full inclusion — the practice of educating students with special needs in the regular classroom as much as possible. We have witnessed the demise of special classes, the trepidation felt by teachers as their classes changed, and the renewed vigor that grows from collaboration in the classroom with a teacher and a support teacher working together to better meet the needs of all students. It is in this setting that we strive for practices that create a safe and productive learning environment for all.

We have moved from "allowing" students with special needs "in" to welcoming all students and working to build classroom and school communities where everyone feels a sense of belonging and makes academic progress.

What is inclusion?

- Inclusion is the practice of welcoming all students to their neighborhood school.
- It is the practice of educating all children in age-appropriate, heterogeneous classrooms.
- It is the practice of including parents when planning for students.
- It is the practice of working together as a staff to better meet the learning needs of each and every student — whether or not a student has been identified as having special needs.
- And it is the practice of designing programs for children with special needs that rely, as much as possible, on the learning objectives and practices of the regular classroom.

Why value it in schools?

- Education is more than an academic process. We need to develop the brain *and* the emotions and use children's strengths to build academic success.
- Schools provide the advantage of a community. We learn to move beyond a collection of individuals searching for their rights to a welcoming community that works and learns and feels together.
- Students with special needs learn a lot from the modeling of their age-appropriate peers — both socially and academically.
- Non-identified students learn about acceptance and respecting differences. Everyone is reminded that we all learn in different ways and at different rates.
- The world is shrinking dramatically and constantly changing. Schools should reflect and prepare students for the best society we know — the one we want to help create. Surely this is one that respects and values all its members.

What are the core values and beliefs of our model of inclusion?

- All children can learn, albeit in different ways and at different rates.
- All children have strengths, and part of our role as educators is to encourage and highlight those strengths in the classroom.
- Learning is a developmental, active, continuous, constructive process, building on the prior experiences of the learners.
- All children can be included, have the right to be included, and may, indeed, challenge us to make inclusion a positive reality in the class-room and school.
- Parents are part of our educational team. We need their input and we respect and appreciate their involvement.
- School should be a place where all students and staff enjoy a sense of belonging and a belief that they contribute. They should also feel valued.
- Teachers, students, administrators, and paraprofessionals will grow personally and professionally by working together to meet diverse needs.
- Successful inclusionary practices are possible, manageable, and hap-pening in a variety of ways in a variety of places.
- Although a change to more inclusionary practice can be threatening to many, it does not mean taking time away from regular students, low-ering standards, or allowing identified students to "be there, keeping a seat warm."
- Children are the province of the whole school, not one teacher.

How do we begin to be inclusive?

- *Be flexible!* It is the most important characteristic needed by all staff. This flexibility will be called upon in thinking, in planning, and in design-ing support models. These models need to be dynamic, changing as learner needs alter. Listen to the voices of a few inclusive practitioners:

   In my first year here I had more resource room intervention, which certainly took less of my energy because the kids left the classroom. Now with the resource support in the classroom, I need more energy but the results are well worth it.

   — Steve Rosell, teacher

   This inclusive school must have a community feel to it. It is a welcoming school, with a problem-solving kind of atmosphere, where, when concerns, issues, problems develop, rather than throwing our hands in the air, we problem-solve in groups of two or three or whatever. Maybe the key is flexibility....

   What has also been critical is our supporting the classroom teacher [re: a Kindergarten student who "loses" control]. We have had to pull time from other kids and teachers in order to intensify the support for this situation. We talk together about supporting one another. Some teachers don't like it at first, but they also know that we'll be there for them when a critical situation arises.

   — Randy Cranston, consultant

"Don't get me wrong...I'm good, but I'm not great because great takes two."

— Linda Rivet, teacher

- *Be collaborative.* We truly need the expertise of all in order to make the move toward more inclusive practices work. Teachers, parents, and students can collaborate. We need to share our views, pose questions, and listen carefully.

  The best thing about collaboration is that adults learn from each other. It is an ongoing, connected inservice that involves modeling and reflection. This model has most helped one of the authors here refine her skill as a teacher.

  And another teacher, Tammy Wirick, observes: "The best thing about collaboration is that it forces you to question whether what you are doing is best for the children you are working with, and it provides a mirror — it balances your thinking both emotionally and intellectually."

- *Be prepared to problem-solve.* Each student can open a new range of possibilities. The whole school must be a safe place for everyone.

  Working with students with challenging behavior is worthwhile. As one teacher, Linda Wingren, puts it: "The other kids love you too because they see that you never give up on anyone and you include everyone. We can't afford to let go of anyone."

- *Be a planner.* Planning is key. Support personnel must work carefully with parents and classroom teachers to design appropriate educational experiences (to adapt the curriculum) on an ongoing basis. Plans are best established before support personnel join the teacher in the classroom. This does not have to mean a delay in service. Support personnel should be in the classroom early in the term, observing, collecting information, assessing student performance, scaffolding learning, and interacting with the students. Then, armed with pertinent information, the classroom teacher and the support personnel meet to establish their plans, which should be monitored regularly for service to be effective.

  Planning is nine-tenths of the program. One resource teacher, Gina Rae, says that when she and teachers meet "it is a very open process. We prioritize the needs of the class and then make a commitment to act. We plan one term at a time and renegotiate the timetable as we go. The teachers know it is not forever. I keep my timetable available for all the teachers I work with. This helps us be better as a group and helps create a school feeling for all the kids."

- *Be aware of the language used when describing students.* Choice of language is powerful. It influences the thinking of others — that of the students and their parents, as well as that of those who work with the students in school. Always refer to students in positive language. For example, saying "a student with learning disabilities" is more positive than saying "a learning-disabled student." The first focuses on the student, then a specialty, while the second suggests that the disability is more important than the person.

  Stay away from labels. Labels prevent us from understanding students. They limit our ideas of who students are and what they can do. When our thinking falls into stereotypes, we limit students' experiences and response. For example, how can a teacher call a child who isn't performing a non-reader and a non-writer? The task is to find out what is stopping the child and then figure out what to do about it.

- *Be aware of how you spend your time.* Extensive testing prior to providing a program for a student is costly in terms of time and personnel. Vulnerable students should not be left to flounder with the regular classroom curriculum and expectations pending a formal assessment. With support personnel helping the teacher in the classroom, observations of a student's interactions with others can begin immediately. These observations then become the nucleus of a profile of strengths and needs that lead to the necessary programming adaptations or scaffolding. Although a formal assessment might sometimes be required, most planning for student programming is based on ongoing data collection in a variety of learning situations. It is also tied to the curriculum learning outcomes and to classroom experiences. This planning is interactive and closely monitors a student's progress.

   "When I'm in the class I know I'm connecting to the curriculum that's being taught in the classroom," says principal and resource teacher, Randy Cranston. "I can scaffold for the students and teach them the necessary skills.... I also find the students are more motivated when their support occurs in the regular classroom."

- *If you are support personnel, be prepared to play a key role in beginning and maintaining an inclusive focus.* Accurate record-keeping is a mandate. Ongoing dialogue among staff regarding student needs and the effectiveness of the intervention or scaffolding can often be initiated by support personnel. The modeling of positive language about students helps sharpen thinking. You are in a special position when it comes to influencing the growth of a learning community in a school. Remember: Inclusion is not focused on one population. It is making everyone feel that they are important and a part of the school. Behaviors ranging from welcoming to encouraging and from supporting to problem-solving are all practiced in a strong community. Students can capitalize on the social aspects of learning and, as members of a community, share the highs and lows of the individuals within it.

Why does the connectedness of the group matter?

The importance of inclusion, as advocated here, is that parents, students, and staff all have a voice and feel they are a part of a strong community. It can be seen as being part of a team. Teachers who teach in ways that include all students find that their classrooms change. Naryn Searcy, a secondary teacher, eloquently sums up what she has found: "The community becomes richer and it becomes more inclusive. Many students have strengths and talents that we never see in our classrooms because there is no place for them to show them. Students now take notice of other's strengths, learning things about each other that they never knew before, encouraging and supporting each other, and learning to respect each other in new ways."

Part One

Building an Inclusive School

1

Developing a School-wide Code of Conduct in Elementary and Middle Schools

At our school we take pride in
- caring for and including others
- respecting people
- respecting and caring for property
- showing safety for self and others

— Draft of school code of conduct

Schools are complex places. Students, teachers, staff, administrators, parents, and often community members interact daily. Each school develops a particular culture.

Some schools let their culture develop on its own; other schools take steps to promote a culture that they value. In the latter instance, they seek to make the culture explicit to all members of the school community. One way of doing this is to develop a school code of conduct based on beliefs rather than rules.

Developing a school code of conduct is a process. It is *not* just a matter of adopting another school's code. Some schools involve students and the larger school community in developing their code. If the staff believes that inclusion of all members of the school community is important, then they will invite those members of the community to take part. This invitation can be stated explicitly in the staff's philosophy that all belong, all need to be welcomed, and all have something to contribute. A school that wants to build this kind of culture will work through a time-consuming — but rewarding — process.

We recommend that a school code encompass all school community members. When you develop a code of conduct that *explicitly* states that all students, staff, and parents/guardians belong, then you have a strong foundation statement to refer to when talking with students and adults about instances where certain members are excluded.

What follows is a process developed in one elementary school and used by many others. The outcomes of this process are particular to one school. Another school using the process would develop a different set of outcomes.

Establishing the Process

In our province, all schools are required to develop a school-wide code of conduct. Schools use many different processes to do this: some involve staff only; some, staff and students; others, a wider group of people. Some base their code on rights and responsibilities, others on rules, and others on beliefs.

One elementary staff decided to give everyone in the school community an opportunity to provide input into the school code of conduct. They decided to develop a long-term process that would take a year to implement and a lifetime to reinforce!

The teaching/administration staff met on a professional development day and decided that they wanted to

1. develop a code that was meaningful, understandable, easily referred to, and based on beliefs not rules
2. have students, parents, and non-professional staff take part in the process in order to develop ownership of the school code
3. develop a process that was meaningful to all members of the school community

They made the decisions knowing that having everyone involved in the process would encourage ownership. They believed that, if they were truly striving toward being an inclusive community, then all members needed to be part of establishing the philosophy and beliefs that would become the foundation for decisions made in the community.

They also recognized that involving more people would take more time.

Implementing the Process

1. *The Public Invitation*
   A school newsletter and a parent advisory council meeting invited parents to join with students and staff at a school assembly to begin the process of developing a school code of conduct.

2. *Assembly for Students, Staff, and Parents*
   The school held an opening assembly that focused on
   • a desire to build a caring and inclusive community
   • the need to develop a code of conduct based on the beliefs of how we should treat each other rather than a set of rules on how we should behave

   A question was posed to everyone: "What makes you feel safe and cared for at school?" With this question in mind, students, parents, and staff divided into groups of nine to twelve, each with an adult facilitator (teacher or parent). Each group was asked to brainstorm and record what made them feel safe and cared for at school. The session lasted ten minutes. If the brainstorming slowed, the teacher facilitators stimulated thinking through these questions:

   How do you like to be treated?
   How do you think you should be treating others?

How should property and things such as books and computers be looked after?
How do we keep ourselves and others safe?
What makes you feel good about school?
What does caring look like?
How would we want to treat adults coming into the school?

Once response cards were collected, the students were told they would be doing further work with the ideas in their classrooms. Parents were invited to meet in the staffroom with the principal to look at a variety of codes of conduct from other schools and to get a picture of what it was they were helping to develop.

3. *Classroom Work*
Each classroom was given approximately fifty cards. Their task was to sort and categorize the cards into five categories and come up with a name for each of these categories. The students were asked to try to develop at least one category name that no other group would likely come up with. The teachers found the strategy was successful with all grade levels. The charts of categories were then displayed in the hallways.

4. *The Second Assembly (one week after the first)*
Students, staff, and parents again gathered in the gym. Each class presented their charts of categories and read out the five category names. Category titles included such names as Put ups, No Breaking Hearts, Friendships, and Things We Want. The five categories from all of the classrooms were listed on the overhead and copies of this list were given to each classroom.

5. *Classroom Work*
Students worked to narrow all the category names to about five categories.

6. *The Third Assembly*
Students, staff, and parents gathered again. Each class presented their smaller list of categories. Some older students presented scenarios of student behavior on the playground to highlight some of the category names that they had developed. For example, one group did a skit illustrating respect and disrespect for school property.

7. *Special Classroom Task*
One intermediate classroom volunteered to take the category names and put them into the following general categories:

respectful behavior — respect people
respect property
friendship — keeping friends
no breaking hearts — including people
things we want (safety)
safety — a right to feel safe
respect for our school
helping

8. *Staff–Parent Meeting*

   Staff and parents met to refine ideas further. They developed these points:

   > At our school we take pride in
   > - caring for and including others
   > - respecting people
   > - respecting and caring for property
   > - showing safety for self and others

9. *Student and Parent Forums*

   Students in all the classrooms and parents at a parent advisory council meeting took all the cards that had been written at the first assembly, to ensure they would fit into one of these four categories.

   The full code of conduct then read as follows:

The _____ Elementary School community believes that it is important to establish a warm, supportive environment. We do this by

- caring for and including others
- respecting people
- respecting and caring for property
- showing safety for self and others

Our code of conduct applies to all members of the _____ community. We use our code to teach and encourage positive behavior.

Actions that do not respect our school code of conduct will result in appropriate consequences.

The final two lines were added because district policy required the inclusion of something of this nature. However, over the last several years, lines like these have changed for many schools as they learn more about Restorative Practices. In those schools, the final two lines have changed focus: "Whenever possible, incidents will be resolved by discussion, mediation, and restitution. Every effort to support students and to determine the root causes of behavior will be made." This part of the code is much more positive and reinforces that the staff is working with students to learn more about their behavior, to take responsibility for it, and to fix their mistakes.

The code of conduct was distributed widely. It was printed and posted around the school and put on large boards and displayed on the playground and on the outside wall of the gymnasium, where it could be seen by people visiting the school. Parents were sent copies through the school newsletter and were thanked for their involvement.

Reflecting on the Process

Having a code of conduct that was developed by the staff, students, and parents successfully encouraged ownership. Student voices were heard at each step. Adult input, as in the case of refining the final list of categories, was added only after the ideas had been developed by the students. If the final code was truly to reflect the philosophy of school community members, it had to make explicit the foundation of beliefs of the school community. For example, the code of conduct at this school explicitly reflects inclusion when it says "caring for and including others." This phrase gives students, staff, and parents something to speak to if they feel that they or other members of their school community are not being included.

Developing a code is only the beginning. Time, instruction, and discussion must accompany the code if students, staff, and parents are to live by the code. Keeping the code alive means calling upon the school community to reflect constantly on their beliefs and values — and then to "walk the talk."

Keeping the Code Alive

There are many ways to keep the code alive and meaningful. In this book, there are chapters about belonging, choice, and teaching so all kids can learn. All these ideas help reinforce the code of conduct that talks about respect, inclusion, and safety. As a teacher, you have to make those connections for the students. The Annotated Bibliography of Classroom Resources on page 143 offers suggestions for materials and resources that can be used to help the teach the code. Following are several concrete ways to reinforce the code and its values:

1. Set up monthly meetings of multi-age groups to do activities related to the school code. Possible activities are
   - *illustrating each part of the code with different forms of art.* These representations can be displayed in the school or presented at assemblies.
   - *using a "pieceful strategy" to illustrate what each part of the school code really means.* For example, putting together a puzzle shape in the form of a heart to represent "caring and including others"; putting together a puzzle shape in the form of a school building to represent "respecting and caring for property." Again, these representations can be presented or displayed to make the thinking behind the code more accessible for all students.
2. Hold monthly assemblies where classes take turns presenting role-plays, skits, songs, poems, and readings that bring to life parts of the code.
3. Use the language of the code explicitly in every situation. For example, when introducing a visiting drama group to a school assembly, you might say, "We'd like to welcome the Tropedoors, and show

them how well we live by our school code by being a very respectful audience who will help them feel included in our school community."

4. Honor the parents, staff, and students who help make the school a safe and caring place to be. When comments are made about the contributions of noon-hour supervisors, the custodian, patrol parents, office staff, and library monitors, they are explicitly connected to the parts of the code of conduct.

5. Teach and reteach the code each year:

   • *Do T-charts*. Explore what respect for others looks like, sounds like.

RESPECT FOR OTHERS

Looks Like	Sounds Like
people listening to each other	Please, thank you
eye contact	I like your _____
holding open the door	That's a great _____
helping someone if hurt	compliments
taking turns	encouraging...

   • *Introduce carousel brainstorming*. Write each section of the code on different pieces of chart paper and have students brainstorm what you would see if everyone in the school community was living by the code. If everyone was "showing safety for self and others," what would you see? A sample response for respecting property also appears here:

SHOWING SAFETY FOR SELF AND OTHERS	RESPECTING PROPERTY
going down the slide the right way	picking up litter
taking turns on the equipment	taking care of library books
	pushing chairs in
	asking before borrowing

   • *Develop People Searches*. Work with multi-age groups or individual classes. (See Appendix 1 on page 138 for more on the strategy.) Ask students to find someone who can describe certain aspects of the school code. They might work with a form with directions such as these:

Find someone who

- can tell you why we have a
  school code of conduct:

- can describe three ways
  they respect and care for
  property:

- can describe a time when
  they felt they were
  included:

- can imagine what it would be
  like if everyone in our school
  felt they belonged:

- can tell you about a time
  when they helped someone
  stay safe:

- can think of two things they
  can do today to help others
  feel they belong:

- *Institute reflection journals.* Each week students and staff can reflect on the code of conduct through writing or drawing. Here are some specific ways of jogging reflection:

  Create a compliment tree for someone in the school community.
  Draw a map of your heart and label the parts.
  Collect data on the respectful language that students in your classroom use.
  Write/draw four random acts of kindness you could try this week.

The chart on page 18, Summary of the Process Used in Developing a Code of Conduct, outlines the inclusive process used for creating a code of conduct that will reinforce the desire for a safe school where all members of the community enjoy a sense of belonging.

Summary of the Process Used in Developing a Code of Conduct

Staff meets to develop process

|

- parents are invited to join staff and students at assembly to introduce process

|

First Assembly
- songs and poems emphasizing caring and community and the desire to build a caring and inclusive community
- introduction of development of a code based on beliefs
- participants are divided into small groups to brainstorm:
  What makes you feel safe and cared for at our school?

|

Classroom Work
- each classroom takes approximately 50 cards and sorts and categorizes these cards into 5 categories
- students name each category
- charts are hung in the hall for everyone to see

|

Second Assembly: one week later
- songs
- each class presents their 5 category names

|

Classroom Work
- each class works to narrow all the category names down to 5 categories

|

Third Assembly
- songs
- shorter list of categories presented
- older students present skits to demonstrate some categories

|

- one classroom takes all category names and narrows them into a short list of categories

|

- staff meets to refine list further

|

Parent Meeting/Classrooms
- take original cards from first assembly and categorize the cards into the refined categories to ensure all items will fit into one of these categories

|

Final Code

|

- teach/reteach
- *keep code alive*

Pembroke Publishers © 2011 *Learning in Safe Schools, revised edition* by Faye Brownlie and Judith King ISBN 978-1-55138-266-1

2

Building a Culture Where All Students Belong

co-authored with

KIM ONDRIK

with input from Rhonda Staples, Deb Webster, and Lorraine Hanson

"A seed holds an incredible life force. When conditions are right, the seed bursts, sending forth an embryo root and stem. Each time, the same thing happens with mind-boggling regularity. *But the key to the process is to give the right seed the right conditions — which is the gardener's job.*"

— Gerald Knox, gardening authority

"From my belonging research I have learned that this simple idea is at the core of every person. It's the soil from which a seed grows... belonging is to learning as soil is to a seed."

— Kim Ondrik, teacher

Fostering a culture of "belonging" in a community can help children develop love, friendship, commitment, and caring. This "belonging" moves students to act in an inclusive way, change behavior, go out of their way for others, and appreciate others for who they are.

How deeply these changes happen in the classroom seems to depend on the individual teacher: how much the teacher cares about developing an inclusive culture, how able he or she is at reaching individual students, and how involved he or she allows students to be in developing that community. Teachers who value a culture where everyone feels they belong set it as a priority, and constantly model respect and caring in their behavior and language. Many teachers believe, though, that a strong culture is more easily built when they have same students for a few years.

The "Journey" outlined on page 20 is an example of the work of a teacher who cared about establishing a culture of belonging in her primary multi-aged classroom.

The Need to Belong as the Soil for Learning

The term "belonging" was coined by A. H. Maslow and appears with "love" on his hierarchy of needs. Maslow put forth the premise that human beings are motivated to satisfy needs. These needs are hierarchical and must be at least partially satisfied before a person will try to satisfy higher needs.

One critical concept introduced by Maslow was the distinction between deficiency needs and growth needs. Deficiency needs (physiological needs, safety, love, and esteem) are those that are critical to physical and psychological well-being. These needs must be satisfied, but once they are, a person's motivation to satisfy them diminishes. In contrast, growth needs, such as the need to know and understand things, to appreciate beauty, or to grow and develop an appreciation of others,

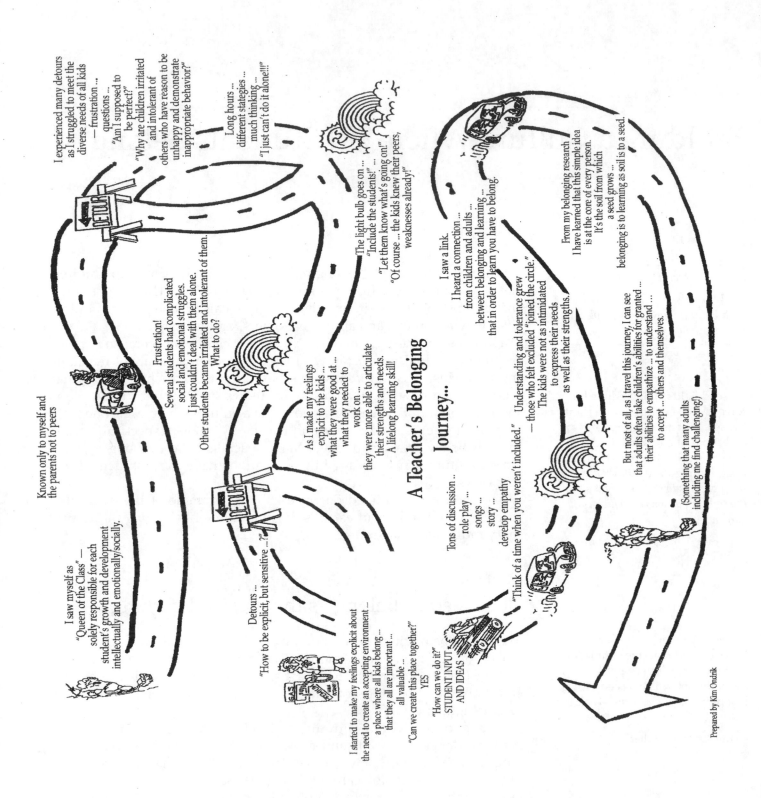

A Teacher's Belonging Journey...

Prepared by Kim Ondrik

20

can never be satisfied completely. In fact, the more individuals can meet the need to know and understand the world around them, the greater their motivation may become to learn more.

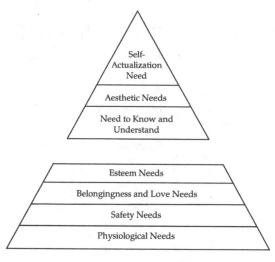

Maslow's Hierarchy of Needs

At school, we generally focus too narrowly on satisfying growth needs, developing children's intellectual skills. The problem is that children who are hungry or who come from abusive situations will have very little psychological energy to put into learning. They have many more basic needs to satisfy before they can grow intellectually. Similarly, if children do not feel accepted or included in a classroom, they are unlikely to have a strong motivation to achieve the higher growth objectives — the search for knowledge and understanding for their own sake, or the creativity and openness to new ideas. A child who is unsure of his or her acceptance in a class may feel sad or rejected, make the cautious choice, go with the crowd, or study for a test without any interest in learning the ideas.

If a teacher can create a classroom where all children feel they belong, in Maslow's view, the students will become eager to learn for the sake of learning. Children will also open themselves to new ideas and take creative risks. If they are to become self-directed learners, children must feel that they are loved, that the teacher will respond to them fairly and consistently, and that they will not be ridiculed or punished for honest answers or risk taking.

"If you belong, you learn more... you won't be worried."

— A primary student

Classrooms built on the philosophy of belonging have caring, safe environments where children support and help each other. Such a philosophy promotes an "I can" attitude in all children. When children feel they belong, they feel safe and secure and good about themselves. As a result, they become tolerant of others, more accepting and forgiving.

Classrooms that foster a sense of belonging provide an environment that encourages risk-taking, allows for a cooperative spirit, models acceptance, encourages divergent thinking, promotes appreciation of others, practices empathy, and recognizes the unique contributions that each individual makes to the group. Safe classrooms provide for effective exchanges between individuals. Safe classrooms are warm, loving, caring, and honest.

Establishing a Framework for Teaching Belongingness

"...if you find that you don't have ideal or even good soil, you don't have to be satisfied with what you have. You can improve it to help make sure your plants feel at home."

— Gerald Knox

Four understandings must be in evidence before the teaching of belongingness can take hold.

1. Make the concept explicit

Belonging is a curriculum on its own. It has to be taught as life skills. It can't be treated as a theme that can be covered in a few weeks. This belonging curriculum has its own vocabulary that the children need to learn in order to communicate effectively.

"Belonging" should become a classroom word. Teachers need to talk about belonging with their students and bring the subtleties out into the open, letting the children become aware of what they do to promote it. Discussions centred around belonging make implicit social behaviors and feelings *explicit*.

The language of belonging is striking — *love, care, value, important, share, help, encourage, friendship, support, freedom, choices, problem-solving*. As students begin to understand the concept, their language becomes *descriptive* — "What does belonging feel like, look like, and sound like?" Their language also becomes *prescriptive* — "What can you do so everyone belongs?"

2. Include children in problem-solving

"When you solve the little problems then you don't have big problems."

— Robert, Grade 2

Discipline problems are minimized when children understand the feelings of others and can better relate those feelings to their own experiences. In a classroom where belonging is emphasized, difficulties become everyone's problem. Everyone is responsible for the solutions. Fingers are not pointed and children are not singled out. Everyone works together to re-establish the feeling of belonging, giving the child ownership over the problem and a sense of empowerment from being part of the solution. By discussing belonging in the classroom, children's problem-solving skills are enhanced in a meaningful way.

3. Teach inclusion — and celebrate diversity

Belonging allows for and celebrates diversity. A strong sense of belonging can transcend any unease created by diversity — physical, mental, and cultural. Talking about belonging and what is important helps children realize that it's their "heart condition," how they treat themselves and others, that matters, not how many toys they own, or how many different clothes they have, or how quickly they learn something new.

4. Establish a relationship with each child

Children need a relationship with the adult in the classroom to get their bearings, to understand what is acceptable and not acceptable, to observe and emulate. They need to be able to transfer the relationship they have with their parents to their teacher, to know they are accepted, *safe*, and cared for. "Once there is a strong connection between adult and child, the child will respond to the tiniest cues from the adult," says child psychologist Gordon Neufeld. Penelope Leach, in *Children First*, writes that "Children depend on parents or their substitutes not only to maintain their self-esteem but also to build it." She believes that teachers need to play the role of the "parent substitute" and not be detached from students. She says further that teachers must be "involved in reciprocal interpersonal relations" with students, not see students as "objects to be taught if they will listen, controlled rather than consulted if they will not."

Concrete Ways to Create a "Belonging" Classroom

You can begin to create a genuinely inclusive classroom through discussions and activities, such as are outlined below. The examples here deal with younger children, but can easily be adapted for students through middle school and, in some cases, for secondary students. For other ideas for middle and secondary grades, see chapters 5–7, where the ideas presented here are pursued in a variety of ways for use with older students.

1. Brainstorm "What is belonging?" We prefer to begin with whole-class brainstorming, moving to individual responses, which honor each child's contribution. An example appears below.

A place where I belong
is _____
because_____
A place where I don't belong
is _____
because_____

I belong outside with my friends.

2. Ask students to reflect on where they feel they belong and why — and where they don't. This activity can be done using various formats at any grade level or using cross-grade buddies. One option is to provide open-ended sentences such as those in the margin at left.

What does a classroom where all kids belong look like, sound like, and feel like?

What does a classroom where belonging is not thought about look like, sound like, and feel like?

people that have hatd hatts and people don't make peopls Belong.

3. Explore these two questions with your students: (1) What does a classroom where all kids belong look like, sound like, and feel like? (2) What does a classroom where belonging is not thought about look like, sound like, and feel like?

How One Primary Multi-Age Class Addressed Questions on Belonging

What does belonging look like in our classroom?

- painting together
- playing together (playground, swings)
- going down the slide together
- making pictures, coloring together
- building something with friends
- sharing a book
- helping me at cleanup time
- working in groups...

What does belonging sound like in our classroom?

- come and play
- I like you
- I'll play with you. Do you want to play?
- Do you want to come to my house?
- You are a good friend
- You have lots of detail in your picture
- That is awesome
- Thank you. You are welcome...

What does it feel like when you belong?

- good
- warm and cozy
- comfortable
- caring and loving
- safe
- fun and happy
- soft
- kind

What does it feel like when you don't belong?

- scary 'cause I might get hurt
- sad
- hurt
- anxious
- mad, angry
- uncomfortable
- lonely, left out
- worried
- like I'm in danger

4. Ask students to consider whether belonging helps them learn "school things." How does it do this? In a primary multi-aged classroom, the children seemed to connect *not belonging* to a preoccupation with

problems that need to be solved, or with worry and anxiety. "If you don't belong then you worry." "If you belong, you get more work done." "You can ask for help so you learn more!" "It's good to belong in the classroom because if you have a problem, you can't focus on your work — you keep thinking about your problem."

5. Invite students to respond to each triad of prompt statements below. They can tell their stories or draw their answers. See Appendix 2 on page 139 for strategy.
   a) Think of a time when you belonged.
      Think of a time when you didn't belong.
      Think of a time when you made someone feel like they belonged.
   b) Think of a time when you weren't included.
      Think of a time when you saw someone not being included.
      Think of a time when you didn't include someone.

   Once through the process, pull the class together to reflect on what they learned from one another and how they can put these ideas into action.

6. Ask students to show, through drawing, when someone belongs and when they don't.

7. Every once in a while do a heart check and see how students are feeling about life in the classroom. This activity is a great starter for class discussions.

8. Introduce *Thinking Yes, Thinking No* to your students. Give each student a page divided in half. Ask students to think of a time they felt loved, cared about, and included, then to think of a time they felt left out, alone, out of place. Before they begin their individual work, invite students to share some reflections with the whole class so they can get an idea of what others are thinking. For younger students who are new to the concept of belonging, you might connect the feelings of happiness and sadness to belonging and not belonging.

   The students draw and write about feeling included on the first half of the paper and share their thinking with a partner. Later, some students can share their reflections with the whole group. Repeat the process, having the students draw, write, and talk about not feeling included.

   After the children have finished the task, try to push their thinking. Ask them to describe why they felt the way they did. For example, "Kenny, what was it about going swimming with your friends and family that made you feel that you belonged?" or "When the boy teased you, how did you feel? What was it about that that made you feel you didn't belong?"

   As the students describe specifically what made them feel they belonged or didn't belong, record their thinking in two columns:

Reflective "Heart Check"

Getting these ideas from my brain was ... great because
I just knew what
I was going to paint
in my head
I felt like I belonged today

in the class   ♡ ♡ ♡

on the playground   ♡ ♡ ♡

25

Happy or Belonging	Sad or Not Belonging
special time	alone
listened to	hurt feelings
somebody helped me	nobody cared

9. Make a large heart out of rolled paper, perhaps 1.5 metres (4.5 ft.) by 1.5 metres (4.5 ft.). Cut it into jigsaw pieces so that there are enough pieces for each person in your room. Discuss with students what makes them feel they belong at school or in the classroom. Give each student one puzzle piece to draw and write on. Have the class work together to make the heart shape. This heart can serve as a meaningful visual representation of what the class believes in and is working toward.

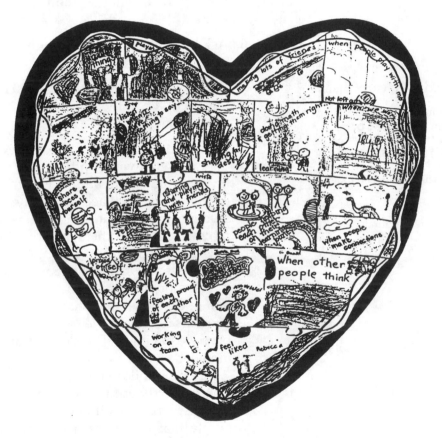

10. Have students write about their Belonging Journey as described in chapter 4.

11. Use literature to reinforce and spark further discussion about belonging and not belonging. For example, you might work with *The Very Best of Friends* by Margaret Wise and Julie Vivas.
    • Have the students predict the story from the title.
    • Choose four pictures from the book that show emotion, or examples of belonging and not belonging. Reduce the four pictures and

copy them onto one sheet of paper. Make one photocopy for every two students. Have students work in pairs and cluster around the pictures their ideas about the images, or the story.

- Give the students four words from the story, for example: "lonely," "meowed," "snuggled," and "heart." Have the students illustrate the four words.

- Direct students to write a prediction of what the story will be about or a short story based on the book title, pictures and clusters, and the four vocabulary words.
- Read the story to the students. Stop in several places and discuss whether or not the characters are feeling they belong or don't belong. After completing the story, have students, as a group, gather evidence as to why the characters felt they belonged or didn't belong.

One summary appears below.

Belonging	Not Belonging
they are together	cat had to stay outside
they love their cat	Jessie is alone in the house
the cat snuggles on the bed	bolted the flap
man and cat stay together	William stopped doing all the familiar things
the man and woman snuggle	cat scratches Jessie
the food bowl, flap in the door	

- Read the story again. In the large group, invite students to identify and record heavy-hearted and happy-hearted words. Talk about the implications of using such words in the classroom and build a T-chart of happy- and heavy-hearted words used there.

Happy-hearted Words	Heavy-hearted Words
loved, together, best of friends, happy, friends, pleased, snuggled, purred	alone, scratches, crossly, dreadful, cried, dark, lonely, yowled

An annotated bibliography of other suitable books is featured at the back of this book.

12. Create People Searches that focus on the concepts of belonging that you have been discussing. Directions for this strategy appear in Appendix 1 on page 138. You might ask students to find people who can do the following:
   - imagine what a school would look like if all of the children felt they belonged
   - name three ways they help others have a happy heart
   - describe what cooperation means
   - explain what "building other kids up" means
   - tell you what belonging means to them
   - explain why belonging is important to them
   - remember a time they didn't belong

Find a researcher who can tell you . . .

People help Together DIS	because if People didn't belong They would be swallowed BRYAN
what belonging means to them	why belonging is important in life
at my other School	
when they didn't belong cristina	

When all of the students have completed their sheets, meet as a group to hear and discuss some of the answers. You might want to record some of the variety of answers on a master sheet.

13. Explore the theme of belonging through art, music, and drama. Have students create art projects that depict belonging or inclusiveness. An example of "rip art," done in red, blue, black, and yellow, appears here. Students were asked to create a large picture representing what belonging meant to them, and to write on the art any words that helped to create the whole picture.

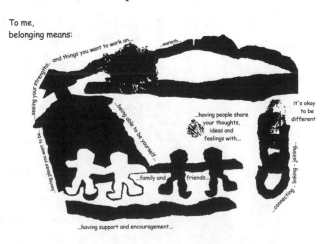

Teach songs and poems that focus on diversity, inclusion, celebration of differences, challenges, problem-solving, and acceptance. *If You Could Wear My Sneakers* by Sheree Fitch is one example. You will find others in the Annotated Bibliography.

Use role-play and role drama to assist students in understanding and sorting through the dilemmas of tolerance, prejudice, friendship, and exclusion.

Practical Ways to Help Parents Understand the Concept of Belonging

If we want parents to reinforce and extend the concept of belonging at home, then we need to provide them with an opportunity to understand and experience what inclusion means. Parents need to know why the teacher is doing what she or he is doing, and be given an opportunity to ask questions, observe, and figure out belonging for themselves.

Teachers who welcome parents into their classroom for purposeful and meaningful reasons extend this feeling of belonging. These parents will experience first-hand some of the benefits of creating this kind of culture. However, just as it is important to teach the students explicitly, it is also important to do the same with parents. Teachers will need to articulate their philosophy to the parents and show consistent evidence of it through an open-door policy. They will need to make personal connections and invitations, encouraging parents to be part of their child's education and classroom. Sending home informative newsletters and holding parent nights that model classroom culture are also constructive.

One teacher held a parent night and invited parents to come with their children. The parents were each given a People Search (see Appendix 1 on page 138) with questions about the culture of the classroom. For example, they were directed to find someone who could explain what belonging means to them, or could tell them three ways to include others. Parents were asked to move around the room, asking students to help them with the People Search. Not only did this put the children in the role of expert, it modeled for the parents what learning looked like in this safe and productive environment.

"Belonging — connected — appreciated — supported...These are feelings essential for success. In a truly inclusive classroom, all students are welcomed and invited to participate in all learning activities. The freedom to create and apply evolving understandings in a risk-free, relevant environment paves the pathway to learning."

— Gladys Rosencrans, district coordinator, special programs

Reflections on Belonging

Explicit teaching of the concept of belonging opens dialogue in the classroom that enables students to talk about how they feel and allows others to care for them. It becomes okay to talk about personal feelings. Children can be heard reassuring others, as in one case when a child said, "No one cares about me," and another six-year-old replied, "I do, Jesse, I care about you."

As students learn about and value belongingness, they become more articulate about what it means to them:

- "I like it when people listen to me, and when they listen I belong there."
- "I am a maker of friendships. I make places where everybody belongs."
- "I used to feel mad, sad, frustrated, . . . now I feel great because I can learn more because I belong."

Belongingness relates closely to emotional intelligence. Daniel Goleman has written that, to him, emotional intelligence is the true indicator of those who live rich and productive lives. He says emotional intelligence encompasses self-awareness and impulse control, persistence, zeal and self-motivation, empathy, and social deftness.

We believe that, in striving for classrooms where belonging is a given, teachers can enable more and more students to grow within their emotional intelligence. As a result, they can live — and learn — more productively, and our society will thrive.

3

Learning as a Journey

co-authored with

KIM ONDRIK
*with input from Rhonda Staples,
Deb Webster, and Lorraine Hanson*

"Babies are born already pro-grammed with a map of the long and complex route towards maturity and beyond, and with the drive to travel along it. The route is the same for every child in the world but the scale of the map is too small to show the millions of minor roads and scenic routes, diversions and disasters, roadblocks and resting places that make each developmental journey unique with unimaginable human diversity. Just as a road map states total distances between major cities but neither predicts nor prescribes individual journey times, so the developmental map is confined to neurobiological distances between sequential landmarks. Babies cannot dance before they run, run before they walk..."

— Penelope Leach, child psychologist

In this chapter, we present a whole-class strategy that will help students to understand that we all have strengths and all have areas to work on. Our goal is that children will honor their own strengths and needs, and the differing strengths and needs of those around them. We want children to realize that learning is a process, not a race. Learning and success can be defined without resorting to making comparisons.

To reflect the concept of learning as a process, we chose the metaphor of a Journey. This concept links to the world outside the classroom because human beings are constantly learning new and different things. We are all on lifelong learning journeys, each going at our own pace.

The Journey metaphor allows students to replace discussions about "who's the best" with commentaries on "my learning journey in math" or "my learning journey in cooperating." At times, students might make observations such as "I feel like a sports car when I'm learning reading," or "I feel like a snail when I play soccer." Just as travelers take different modes of transportation to get to where they want to go, the students will discover that all of their learning journeys are unique. Removed, then, are the strong and damaging comparisons made between students.

When learning is seen as a journey, movement along the continuum becomes the goal. Each student has a goal to keep moving on his or her journey, whether artistic, emotional, intellectual, physical, or social. The concept of the learning journey acknowledges the strengths, needs, and development of every student — we all have things we are good at, and we all have things we need to work on. It is important that, while on their journeys, everyone moves along the continuum of development, feels good about their accomplishments, and has some fun in the process.

Classrooms that focus on learning journeys become communities of learners who do not tolerate put-downs, sarcasm, or comments that imply that because you are having difficulty you are stupid, and because you do it easily you are smart. Instead, they focus on encouraging others to try again, lend a hand, cooperate, use personal strengths to help others, and value and respect individual differences.

In order to create this type of classroom, the teacher must first embrace the idea that learning is a process and that all members of the classroom are on unique journeys. The teacher then needs to focus on building a rich community where individuals help fuel each other's journeys.

Ways to Introduce the Concept of Learning Journey

We have introduced the concept of Learning Journey to students of all ages but in slightly different ways. Even in the classes we have taught at the university level we have introduced the concept and had the students document their journey through the course. There are many different ways to get students thinking about learning journeys. You can use class discussions, small-group work, and individual reflections. Explore some relevant questions with your students. You want them to realize that we learn some things very quickly, other things very slowly. What matters is the forward movement.

1. What is a journey? What words do we associate with journey? What happens on journeys? What are they like? Below is a web that an early primary class brainstormed.

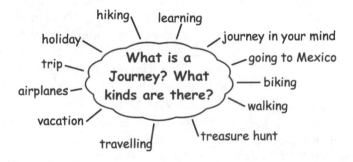

2. We know we all look different from one another. Do you think that we feel and learn differently too? Why or why not?

3. Are we smart at everything or slow at everything? What kinds of things are you quick to learn, and what kinds of things take you more time?

4. If you think of yourself as a lifelong learner, which matters more — speed or movement? Why do you think that?

5. How do you think we learn? Fast like a racecar, slow like a turtle, or at some other pace?

6. We are good at some things and need to work on other things. What is something you are good at? Something you need to work on?

7. Since you are on a journey, consider where you have come from. Where do you want or need to go? Can you chart your journey in reading? in math? in soccer? Where were you in September, and where are you now? (This is the essence of reflection.)

Symbols That Relate to Learning as a Journey

We have found it useful to use symbols that connect with the metaphor of learning as a journey. For younger students these symbols can be made into big posters to be put around the classroom and used in class discussions. You might find it interesting to have older students and students at the college level use these symbols as they describe their learning. There are many different ways to incorporate these symbols.

Roadblocks: What are the roadblocks on your journey? (i.e., reading journey, writing journey, cooperation journey, and so on) What do you need in order to get over/around them?

Fuel/gas station: What will help you to move on your journey? Is there something you need to learn in order to move? Do you need to be encouraged? Do you need assistance?

Uphill: What goals do you struggle to reach? How does that feel? How can others help you get up that hill?

Downhill: What goals have been easy for you to reach? How did that feel? Did others help you?

Carpool: Are you more able to move on your journey if someone helps you? But remember they can't do it for you!

Detour: Do you need to try something else before you can move on your journey?

Illustrations by Riffe Bauman

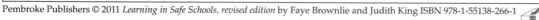
Pembroke Publishers © 2011 *Learning in Safe Schools, revised edition* by Faye Brownlie and Judith King ISBN 978-1-55138-266-1

Beyond exploring many questions to raise students' awareness about learning journeys, plan to provide classroom activities that stimulate discussion and reflection on the topic. Several activities are outlined below.

1. Map out two adults' life journeys (e.g., yours and that of another teacher) on long rolled paper, using the same amount of space for each five years so that you will be able to compare and contrast the journeys. Note some similar events on the two journeys, e.g., first walked, talked, rode a bike, got first job, learned to drive. Then add other life experiences that were significant to each individual (first traveling experience, birth of a child, purchase of a new house, and so on).

    Display the two life journeys. Talk through each journey and point out significant events. Ask the students to compare and contrast the two journeys. In what ways are they similar and in what ways different?

    Look at some specific differences. For example: "Did you notice that Ms. Berezowskyj and I learned to drive a car at different times? I was 16 and Ms. Berezowskyj was 25. Is it okay to learn things at different times? Does it make me smarter than Ms. Berezowskyj because I could drive a car earlier? We all learn some things faster and some things slower. We all have things we are good at and some things we need to work on."

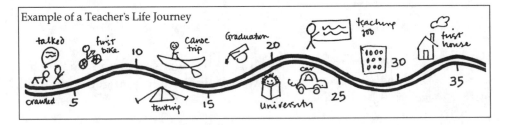

Example of a Teacher's Life Journey

2. Invite students to create their life journeys, noting some similar events (crawling, walking, talking) and then significant moments for each of them. When completed, whole-group and small-group discussions can take place, comparing similarities and differences among children. You can reinforce throughout the discussion the vocabulary and concepts you are trying to introduce: *good at, working on, slow at some things, fast at others, it's okay to learn things at different rates*, and so on.

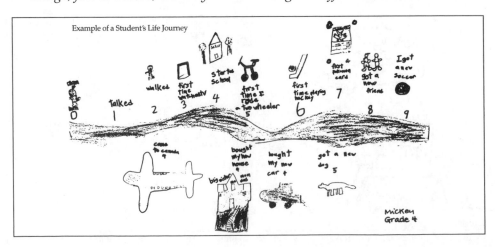

Example of a Student's Life Journey

With a buddy, students can compare their learning journeys and record similarities and differences on a Venn diagram, such as is shown below.

I am good at:

riding my bike without training wheels.

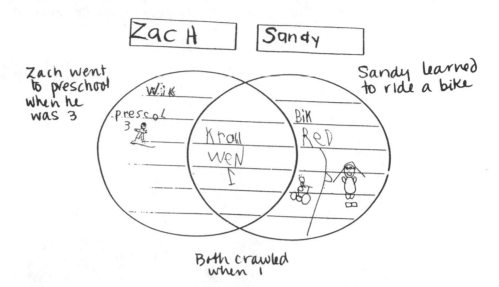

I am working on: SKAT ING

I learn fast like a go-cart.

3. Have students draw and write about things they are good at and things they are working on.

For example: "I was fast at crawling. But I was slow at meeting friends."

4. Ask children to bring in photographs of themselves as babies (the beginning of their life journeys). Then they can reflect on their lives and create webs: "I used to...but now that I am seven, I...."

5. Invite students to come up with similes in response to this question: "On your learning journey, how do you move?"
Here are a few examples:

I can learn slow...like a house tour, like a leaf, like a nail, like a tree trunk, like a brick.

I learn like a cheetah. I can go fast if it's running and slow if it's walking. That's how I learn.

I am journeying like a black tipped shark. I can learn slow, fast, and medium just like the shark moves.

You will see that students readily relate to the idea of learning as a journey. As a result, they feel empowered to use this notion to describe, understand, and reflect upon their learning.

6. Students can apply the concept of learning as a journey to understand and reflect upon their own growth in all areas of their life...writing, reading, friendships, soccer. This ability to reflect and to then plan with the information gained is called metacognition, or thinking about your thinking. In a study of the past fifty years of research on learning, Wang, Haertl, and Walberg list metacognition as the second

most-important factor in helping students learn. (*Educational Leadership* 51(4)).

In the example here, a Grade 7 student set a goal of learning to *solve problems in peaceful ways* (from the B.C. Performance Standards in Social Responsibility). She charted her growth over a four-month period.

Provincial performance standards are useful in tracking changes and in setting goals.

Reflecting on writing journeys is very easy if students use a portfolio collection or a written journal throughout the year. At different points in the year, students can look through their portfolios or journals, note any changes in their writing, and mark these on a writing journey. Students can look at changes in their writing and see their growth over time by looking at things like these: development of BME (beginning, middle, end); connections to feelings and experience; elaborations on ideas; titles; more-complex sentences; punctuation; and descriptive words. After making their journeys, they can set goals for the next term.

"I learned that you do not have to be in school to be able to read and that you learn step by step."

— Student, age 7

7. After much discussion about journeys, you can try to map out a reading journey with your students. Most students are not aware of the milestones involved in learning to read or write. Although they may be aware that they have progressed in their journey, they are probably not aware of what that journey entailed or when it began. For many students, you can either read or you can't read — it's an all or nothing endeavor. Some students don't realize that if they are able to read symbols such as the Big M for McDonald's it is connected with "real reading." The map on page 37, created by a class of seven- and eight-year-olds, reflects a deeper understanding of what constitutes reading.

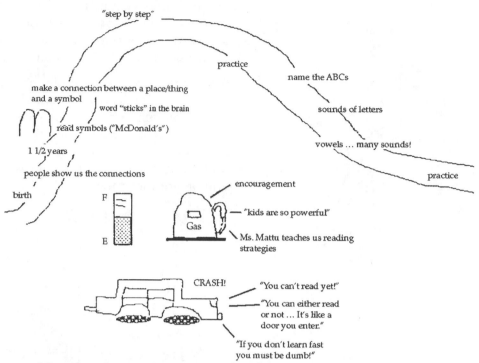

"step by step"

practice

name the ABCs

make a connection between a place/thing and a symbol

word "sticks" in the brain

sounds of letters

read symbols ("McDonald's")

vowels ... many sounds!

1 1/2 years

people show us the connections

practice

birth

F

E

Gas

encouragement

"kids are so powerful"

Ms. Mattu teaches us reading strategies

CRASH!

"You can't read yet!"

"You can either read or not ... It's like a door you enter."

"If you don't learn fast you must be dumb!"

"People read from symbols. You don't just step outside the door and read. It's a journey."

— Student, age 8

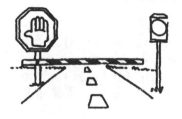

Roadblocks

Fuel

Many students who have been struggling with reading and, consequently, low self-esteem because they believed that they couldn't read, may now gain a fresh perspective. Reading is not something that you can or cannot do. It is a process that begins at birth, and everyone moves at his or her own pace, in his or her own way.

8. Discuss the kinds of things that help or hinder people in their journeys. Talk about how each of us affects each other's journey. We might help others or hinder others by how we respond. For example, what happens if someone laughs at you when you are reading, or makes a comment like "Wow, you sure can't read!"? How do those reactions affect you and your reading journey? And how do you feel when you are trying something new and someone says, "Good for you!" or "Wow, I sure like your painting!"?

Introduce or re-introduce the symbols of roadblock and fuel tank. Brainstorm with the children ways that we help others by fueling up, and ways that we hinder or block others' journeys. Encouragement is fuel for the journey. When people encourage us in our learning, it makes us feel good about what we are doing, and then our brains can relax and learn. Saying something hurtful or discouraging can actually stop people from learning: the brain downshifts into a fight or flight pattern. Research indicates that threatening environments can even trigger chemical imbalances in the brain. As Eric Jensen says in *Teaching with the Brain in Mind*, these "threats activate defense mechanisms and behaviors that are great for survival but lousy for learning." Threats make a roadblock in the brain.

We talk with the children about how often we hurt people's feelings without even thinking about the effect. People might not look

fuel for my journey:

If I was having trouble reading, James could help me by telling me the word I was stuck.

hurt, but inside we may have hurt their hearts and put up roadblocks. Maybe we have stopped them on their friendship journey, running journey, soccer journey, or reading journey. We need to think about what we say and try to be encouraging.

Some questions and activities about fuel and roadblocks:
• What are all the ways you can give fuel to someone?
• Draw yourself giving fuel to someone in your class.
• Draw yourself trying to learn something that is hard for you and show what kind of fuel you would like to get.
• Make a personal web and show ways that others can help or hinder you on your journey.

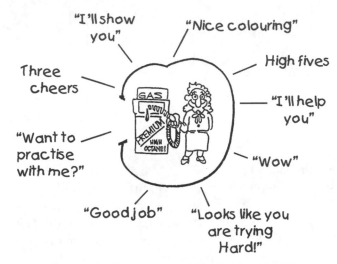

Fuel for the Journey: A Kindergarten Class

Throughout our lives, people put up roadblocks for us. What can we do to help ourselves feel better and stay on our journey without becoming discouraged? Have the class brainstorm for ideas such as encouraging self, talking to a friend, engaging in positive self-talk, ignoring discouraging comments.

9. Review the journey symbols (see page 33). Give an example of a journey of yours to the students and talk about parts of your journey. Show where you had to struggle, what parts were downhill, where you took detours, etc. Have students make up maps of their journeys in many areas. They can use the symbols associated with journeys or describe the things that helped or hindered growth.

10. Explore journeys through literature such as *Thank You, Mr. Falker* or *Mrs. Katz and Tush*, both by Patricia Polacco, or watch a video such as *Homeward Bound*. Map out each character's journey and the ways that others helped or hindered their journey. See the Annotated Bibliography for additional selections.

11. Students in intermediate and secondary classes can apply the concept of the learning journey to the lives of characters in novels they are reading. Using the symbolic icons, they can map the key events of

Doc Smith told Little Willy that grandfather doesn't want to live anymore and doesn't even want to go fishing or to the rodeo.

— Excerpt from a learning journey based on *Stone Fox*

the novel to demonstrate how the character's thoughts, feelings, and actions within the events lead that character to move along a learning journey (Brownlie & Schnellert, 2009; Brownlie, 2005).

12. Role-play and reinforce compliments, "put ups," and other inclusive comments. Doing this helps students reinforce and practice responses, enabling the positive to become more automatic. "If I am discouraged about my journey in soccer, what would you say or do? What could I say and do?"

Reflections on Learning as a Journey

Knowing the concept of learning as a journey is vital. Children need to understand this so they feel better about where they are. Development *is* a process and one that we are on forever, if we so choose. When students understand this, there is a new respect for their own learning processes and that of others. It will not be unusual for them to approach their teachers and parents to ask them about the new things they are learning, or to hear children encouraging each other: "Keep practicing, you'll get it."

As with many of the concepts described in this book, in order to be effective, the teacher must model both the language and the attitudes connected with this concept in daily dealings with the students. If the teacher is expecting all students to do the same work and praises only those who complete it the best, the first, or the tidiest, that teacher is not modeling what process and journeying are all about. If the philosophy of the class is based on competition rather than helping one another, then the idea of journey will not be realized.

The metaphor of learning as a journey fits philosophically within the context of safe, inclusive classrooms — classrooms built with collaboration, open-ended learning methodology, and respect for all individuals as they proceed on their respective journeys.

Part Two

Teaching So All Students Can Learn

4

Planning Lessons with the End in Mind

"In inclusive schools, the focus is not exclusively on how to help students...fit into the existing, standard curriculum of the school. Rather the curriculum in the regular education class is adapted, when necessary, to meet the needs of any student for whom the standard curriculum is inappropriate or could be better served through adaptation. Possibly the most common curricular modification in inclusive schools involves arranging for students to pursue different objectives within the same lesson."

— Stainback and Stainback, authors of *Support Networks for Inclusive Schooling*

Teachers who are working toward a classroom where all students feel they belong and are engaged in learning begin their planning with the end in mind. They determine the key concepts or big ideas for the lesson or lesson sequence, the intended learning outcomes, and the ways students will demonstrate their learning. This is one half of the planning equation. They also consider their students — their strengths, their needs, their interests. With both these considerations in view — students and curriculum — teachers begin to plan the resources, strategies, and support necessary to help all learners achieve success. This is the art and science of effective teaching — bridging the students and the curriculum.

We have found that beginning with the end in mind, also known as Backward Design, is a helpful framework to use when designing learning experiences that include all students. Teachers think of the students in their class, and then begin to plan considering all the learners. Atypical learners are considered from the beginning, not after the lesson or the unit has been designed. Thus, fewer individual adaptations are needed as these considerations are included from the beginning. Often an adaptation included from the planning stage because of a particular student with special needs ends up benefiting other learners (Brownlie and Schnellert, 2009; Brownlie, Fullerton, and Schnellert, 2011).

Teachers who desire to take this approach might find the checklist on page 42 (Checklist for the Teacher Who Values an Inclusive Classroom) helpful.

Below we offer a viable model for planning for productive learning.

A Recommended Planning Model

What are the key concepts that the students are required to learn?

The first critical step is determining the key concepts — the big ideas, the major focus, or a purpose that guides the learning events. Once

Checklist for the Teacher Who Values
an Inclusive Classroom

☐ Are my learning goals clear to the students?

☐ Are my activities open enough so that all students can participate?

☐ Am I using various ways for students to build information and to demonstrate information?

☐ Are there opportunities for students to work alone, in small groups, and as a whole class?

☐ Are my literacy expectations such that most of my students can meet them with support?

☐ Am I varying the way I present material?

☐ Will my sequence allow me time to interact individually with my students?

☐ Have I co-planned with my resource support teacher to help all students accomplish the learning goals?

☐ Will the students be active?

☐ Is there choice for the students in resources, demonstration of understanding, or complexity and abstractness?

☐ Am I co-creating criteria of what success will look like with my students?

☐ Am I providing descriptive feedback (What works? What's not working? What's next?) to students on a regular basis?

Pembroke Publishers © 2011 *Learning in Safe Schools, revised edition* by Faye Brownlie and Judith King ISBN 978-1-55138-266-1

determined, the key concepts serve as a guide as the lessons unfold. Each activity that is then planned will help to make the big ideas clearer to the students.

What specific learning outcomes will be addressed in this lesson or lesson sequence?

Most curricula today are written with learning outcomes clearly stated. However, in too many cases, there are too many outcomes and they have not been prioritized. It is not uncommon for there to be more outcomes than could be achieved by most students in the year. In planning, the teacher reviews the outcomes in the curriculum guide and *chooses* several on which to focus. Sometimes four or five learning outcomes are chosen on which to build the lesson sequence. Learning outcomes can be chosen from several curriculum areas, resulting in an integrated lesson plan. The teacher focuses each lesson, lesson sequence, or unit by stating for the students, "This is what you need to know and to be able to do." These are often stated as "I can..." statements. The outcomes not only guide the learning, but also provide the focus for the assessment. All assessment is based only on what has been taught.

How will the students demonstrate their learning?

Students will need to give evidence that they have achieved the learning outcomes and understood the key concepts of the lesson. Demonstrations of learning should require students to reorganize the material in some way and to connect it to information previously learned. They should also be varied — oral, written, graphic, pictorial, individual, group. Criteria for an effective demonstration can be developed with the students or can be given to the students: many teachers have found that building criteria with students increases student engagement and increases the clarity of the criteria. Working with criteria helps make explicit to all what success will look like.

How will we assess student learning?

The criteria for success, established early in the lesson sequence, needs to be available and visible to the students. Teachers and students use these criteria to monitor their progress and to judge student products or demonstrations. Students should also be encouraged to assess their own work and to set goals for future learning. Two questions focus the students' attention throughout the lesson sequence:

1. What do I need to know?
2. How will I show what I know?

The key concepts, the learning outcomes, and the appropriate demonstration and assessment form the background for the lesson sequence. The next critical step is to paint the foreground. This involves examining the stages in the learning sequence and the type of *support* required at each stage to ensure all learners learn.

Learning Stage 1: Connecting

At this stage, the focus is on what is already known. Prior to the introduction of a new resource, a new topic, or a different point of view, time is spent activating prior knowledge with students: predicting, questioning, writing to learn, sketching, examining specialized vocabulary, connecting the content with real-life stories, examining images or charts. This time of talk, small-group work, question posing, and connecting with self and others is critical to engaging the emotions of students, their curiosity, and their sense of personal relevance, all key factors in learning.

Learning Stage 2: Processing

> "Learning experiences that call forth our feelings and engage our imaginations are more likely to stimulate thought and to last over time."
>
> — Jacquie Dunn, teacher and workshop leader

The focus is on making sense of new information. Strategies at this stage teach students to think about the content being presented, to develop deeper understanding, to read or view interactively, to sort key ideas and align them with supporting details, to connect the new information to their previous understandings and to their questions, and to pose new questions. If students do not actively work with the information, it does not enter their long-term memories or become available for further use.

Learning Stage 3: Transforming or Personalizing

Once the information and experiences have been presented to the students, students need to gain ownership of them, to review and confirm what they have learned. This personal practice sets the students up to use the key concepts in the future and in different contexts. Strategies can include concept maps, drawings, role dramas, writing, or group presentations. Students use their new information to represent what they know in a different way. They work toward meeting the criteria for a powerful demonstration of understanding. Chapter 5 outlines ways you can encourage students to use their strengths in demonstrating their understanding.

The Inclusive Nature of Adaptations

With this planning model, teachers assume that all students will be included. They design sequences and strategies that allow for a range of goal-directed responses. The atmosphere of the classroom acknowledges and honors each learner. Many students who might once have needed individual adaptations no longer need them.

However, there might still be some students who need further adaptations. Consider the group plan: What is to be learned and what is the sequence to facilitate this learning? With this plan in mind, individual adaptations can now be preplanned and quite specific. Where does a given student require support or adaptation? In the environment? In the presentation? In the materials? In assistance? In time? In the goals? In the summative assessment? Some of the adaptations will be lesson-specific, some more long-term. For example, when making an individual adaptation, a classroom or resource teacher might ask these questions:

• "What is the key learning outcome for this sequence/unit?"

- "Which outcomes might the student be more interested in, or able to learn, and in what ways?"
- "How long would I expect most students to take to show they have accomplished learning these outcomes?"

Then, with these questions in mind, the teacher can support the student in choosing a way to demonstrate his or her knowledge of the key outcomes within the same time frame as the rest of the class.

Some students might require Individual Education Plans (IEP). An IEP takes into consideration the student's strengths and needs. The purpose of the IEP is to ensure the student is continuing to progress in the identified areas. In the past, many IEPs have been focused on a deficit model. Using the classroom-based approach presented here, the IEP becomes more strength-based and classroom-focused. More explicit information on designing intervention in this way is found in chapter 8.

In inclusive schools, IEPs are developed collaboratively between the classroom teacher, resource teacher, parent, and, often, the student. They are working documents that guide actions. The IEP looks at ways to assist/support the student in the regular classroom, the place where the student spends all or most of his or her time. The IEP looks at ways that student strengths will be highlighted in the classroom. If the student has good social skills, the teacher ensures that the student recognizes this; if the student is artistic, this strength is highlighted and appreciated. The student's areas of strength can sometimes be used to support the development of needed areas. Ken Robinson states that many people don't know what their strengths/talents are, and that they need others to help them discover them (Robinson, 2001: 25). Teachers are in a position to encourage and appreciate student strengths, and when they do recognize them, students in the classroom will also begin to notice.

IEPs are in contrast to plans that used to outline in detail the child's pullout program, but did not usually deal with the larger period of classroom instruction time. The nature of the IEP reflects a school's commitment to the idea of inclusiveness. If one is to belong in a classroom and be included in a significant way, then collective actions must focus on this. This is the big idea of inclusion.

A Sample Lesson Sequence on the Concept of Belongingness

The following pages demonstrate the planning model outlined earlier in this chapter. Working with two key concepts — belonging, and the impact of our actions on others' feelings — the sample lesson sequence follows the thread from learning outcomes to the final stage of transforming. Showing how a classroom teacher can effectively engage learners of different strengths and abilities while focusing on two key concepts, this teaching is much more explicit than simply reading a great picture book and doing some strategies.

Learning Outcomes: Language Arts, Grade 1/2 (a week of lessons)

Oral Language: Speaking and Listening
• contributing to a class goal
• exchanging ideas on a topic
• making connections

Oral Language: Thinking
• making connections, comparing and contrasting

Reading and Viewing: Thinking
• making text-to-world connections

Writing and Representing: Purposes
• ideas represented through words, sentences, and images that connect to a topic
• developing voice by showing some evidence of individuality
• a logical organization (Grade 2)

Using these Learning Outcomes and knowledge about the students in the classroom, the teacher engages in personal planning to be as prepared as possible to provide inclusive learning experiences through which students can learn productively with appropriate support.

The learning sequence that follows is based on use of the picture book, *Lilly's Purple Plastic Purse* by Kevin Henkes. It is a four-day sequence of lessons focusing on Belonging and the Impact of Our Actions. The teacher has chosen learning outcomes for each lesson and makes these explicit to the students, both orally and on the board.

Day 1: Connecting

GRAB BAG: The Grade 1 and 2 students are seated in their table groups. In front of each student is an 11" × 17" paper, folded into four boxes. The teacher states that they are going to be shown four artifacts from a story that they will read later. These artifacts all relate to the main character. As each artifact is shown to the students, they examine it, then draw how they think it will be used by or with the character in the story. The artifacts are presented one at a time in the following order: (1) a red clicky-heeled shoe, (2) a sharp pencil, (3) a purple purse with three quarters, and (4) a large sign saying "The Lightbulb Lab Where Great Ideas Are Born." There is a wide range of student responses.

One student, Dustin, begins with a boy wearing the red shoes and has him thinking, "I think I will do a tap dance." In his second drawing, the same boy with the tap shoes thinks, "Today I will write about my tap dance." In the third drawing, now including the purse, he thinks, "I will buy some food." Finally, in the last drawing, the Lightbulb Lab has him wonder, "I wonder what they are doing today." Dustin maintains the same character in each drawing, adds on each new artifact, and maintains the same setting of trees and sun.

Learning Outcomes

• I can make connections with a group of artifacts.
• I can show my thinking by drawing.

Dustin's second drawing

Emerald's first drawing

Kelsey's fourth drawing

Another student, Emerald, immediately connects the red shoe to *The Wizard of Oz* and draws Dorothy, the lion, the tin man, and the scarecrow. She adds thinking bubbles in which the lion admits his cowardice and Dorothy says she desires to get to the Emerald City. Emerald has not only connected with her background knowledge, but has added detail to her representation. In her second drawing, the woman wearing the red shoes is in trouble. A thief is running off with her pencil, while the chef yells "Fire!" In the third drawing, Miss Piggy, with her purse, is thinking of her money and wondering aloud what she will write to Kermit the frog, with her pencil. Again, Emerald has applied her prior knowledge and used all three artifacts. Finally, the lady, in her red shoes and with her purple purse, arrives at the door of a mad scientist. It is hinted that she will use her money to buy a "great idea." Emerald predicts, "There was a mad scientist who loved his lab and one day a very rich lady came..."

Finally, a third student, Kelsey, demonstrates a different form of thinking. Rather than work to integrate each new artifact with her budding theory, she makes an abrupt change in her thinking between the second and third artifacts. She began drawing and writing with Pasty the sheep having the prettiest tap dancing shoes in the whole pasture. A prospective customer awaits. In the second box, the pencils are included by adding another character — a magician, who gives Pasty some magic pencils for free. Now the major shift occurs. In the third drawing, Ms. Mulberry is wearing the red shoes and going out with her purple purse to buy pencils, which are being sold for 25 cents apiece. As she is walking home, in drawing four, Ms. Mulberry comes upon a sign for the Lightbulb Lab, so she goes in and gets a new idea.

How this lesson involves all students
All three students have connected the artifacts. All have worked to develop a plausible theory. The degree of sophistication varies; the engagement with the task does not. Dustin has met the basic demands of the task. Emerald has pulled extensively from her background knowledge, forming and abandoning possibilities with each new artifact. Kelsey has begun on one track, then shifted to a completely different theory.

Day 2: Connecting

WRITING FROM THE ARTIFACTS: The students are asked to write a story that includes all the artifacts they saw on the previous day. Dustin begins his story, but needs support in the form of scribing in order to finish. He begins with a known lead, "A long time ago in a far-away land," then moves to rely heavily on the drawings he has already made and on the artifacts. When given the additional support of a scribe, his story becomes more sophisticated, though less tied to the artifacts.

Emerald continues thinking about the mad scientist. She uses all the artifacts, develops a conflict, and resolves it. She also employs conversation.

```
                    Emerald                    DRAFT
Once upon a time ther lived a mad sintist
He loved to werk with his labrotory then a
stormy night a very very ritch lady came
by oh thats just what I need a very
smart bran and she walled into the lab
and she didnot notes the sine but it said
danger on It. Hm hm what will you give
me if I give you a very smart bran
now seed the very ritch lady. Haw ubaut
thows red tap dance shows oh no not my
red dance shows my mother gave me those
shows well haw ubout that pers oh no My
fother gave me that pers well haw ubout
those pensels oh no what will I writ with
if I give you my pensels? Hm hm haw
ubout the money well haw ubout that?
So the very ritch lady got her very smart
bran and the sintist got his money.
The End
```

Kelsey changes her thinking again, as often happens over time. She, too, uses all the artifacts. Kelsey includes conversation, pulls in a dream sequence, and, in so doing, has a story within a story.

How this lesson involves all students
Again all students are engaged. Dustin needs a little support through scribing. Two students work together to create a story.

Day 3: Processing

PREDICTING FROM PICTURES: The students work with partners. They share a large piece of paper that is divided into four boxes. Each box has a picture from the text in it. The story is read to the students, stopping when the picture appears in the text. At this time, the students are invited to work together to decide what is happening in the picture and how the characters are feeling. This process continues for each of the four pictures.

The students' experiences are evident in their predictions. Two girls, Kelsey and Erin, predict that Lilly is drawing differently from the others — a cat, not a mouse — and that this returns to discourage her in box three. Emerald and Stephanie notice the rhymes on the board in the second box, then decide that Lilly is sad because her homework is not done. Dustin and Ben, with help scribing, identify feelings with each picture, including the feelings of another mouse in box two: "He's mad at Lilly 'cause she gets all the good ideas, and she gets picked all the time by the teacher."

Learning Outcomes

- I can share my thinking with a partner.
- I can identify characters' feelings.

48

How this lesson involves all students

Working in partners or triads is an easy adaptation. The issue here is making sure that all students have an opportunity to share their ideas. This requires ongoing explicit teaching.

Day 4: Transforming

HAPPY HEART, HEAVY HEART: The students have now heard the book read aloud. Today, they focus on the three letters that Lilly, the main character, wrote to her teacher Mr. Slinger. The book is reread, stopping at each letter in the book. The teacher guides the whole class by raising questions about the letters. (Copies of each letter can be shown on an overhead, scanned and shown on an LCD projector, or displayed using a document camera.)

Letter 1: Big Friendly Mr. Nice Man Teacher
• How was Lilly feeling when she wrote this?
• How will Mr. Slinger feel if he sees it?
• Which words are happy-hearted words?

Letter 2: Big Fat Mean Mr. Stealing Teacher
• How was Lilly feeling?
• How will Mr. Slinger feel when he gets it?
• Which words would make you feel you don't belong?
• How would you feel if you got this letter?
• Do you think Lilly should have given this to Mr. Slinger? Why or why not?

Letter 3: Lilly was really, really sorry.
• How was Lilly feeling?
• How will Mr. Slinger feel when he gets this?
• Which words are happy-hearted words?
• How would you feel if you were Mr. Slinger?
• What do you do when you feel very, very sorry?

In each case, the questions move from an examination of a piece of text to personal application in response to identified feelings. They help make explicit the feelings of the characters and of the students. This teaching allows students to develop a vocabulary appropriate for expressing their feelings and to appreciate the use of happy-, not heavy-, hearted words. Students will make strides in learning how to include everyone in a risk-free, productive learning environment.

Finally, the students, as a class, web A Happy Heart (see page 50), deliberately focusing on how to act responsibly and how to have every-one in your group belong.

Learning Outcomes

• I can share my thinking in a group.
• I know words to say to help everyone have a happy heart.

Happy-Hearted Words

"for you"
"me too"
lots
jaunty
saved
sharing
loved
special
wink
wow

Heavy-Hearted Words

hard time
not now
fierce
crying
gone
sad
longed
trouble

How this lesson involves all students

This four-day sequence has involved all the students. They have been deeply engaged in working with the text — in analyzing, comparing, discussing, predicting. They have talked, wondered, drawn, written, and read and reread before working as a class to use their interpretation of Henke's work to build a chart of phrases for their class, language that will guide them in their interactions with each other toward building a classroom where all belong. The teacher had a "big idea" when she began the unit — belonging and considering how our actions affect others. She used this big idea to guide her planning, using a group of learning outcomes from the language arts curriculum. She worked slowly, thoughtfully, in a planned way to ensure that the Learning Outcomes were accessible to all and that the big idea, the core content, was as well. All students worked on the same outcomes; some met them in different ways. No one was pulled out for intervention during the sequence.

This chapter has outlined the planning process in a primary classroom. Chapters 6 and 7 outline the long-range planning process that two teachers have used in intermediate and secondary classrooms. All three of these scenarios demonstrate ways teachers work to build a community of learners and teach in such a way that more learners belong and learn.

5

Show What You Know

With thanks to Brian Celli, Andrea DeVito, Myron Dueck, Jeff Fitton, Erica Foote, David Hird, David Kupec, and Naryn Searcy

"Drawing, writing, mathematical notation, musical notation are methods for inquiry, providing alternative ways to know and to express information and emotion. Two or more methods allow the human brain do what it does best: make comparisons between systems of representation. "

— Susan Rich Sheridan

"Those students whose minds work differently — and we're talking about many students here; perhaps even the majority of them — can feel alienated from the whole culture of education. This is exactly why some of the most successful people you'll ever meet didn't do well at school. Education is the system that is supposed to develop our natural abilities and enable us to make our way in the world. Instead, it is stifling the individual talent and abilities of too many students and killing their motivation to learn."

— Ken Robinson (2009: 16)

In many schools, literacy skills continue to be honored more than any other strength that students might have. This does not bode well for learners who struggle with reading and writing. Their other strengths don't necessarily help them to become successful at school.

For the past three years, Judith King has been working with a group of middle and secondary teachers in the Okanagan Skaha School District. These teachers have been explaining *learning* to their students differently from the way it is explained in a traditional classroom. They tell their students that reading and writing are important, but that there are also other effective ways to communicate their thinking. In language arts and in English, students need to continue to improve their ability to communicate through writing, as that is one of the foci of these courses. However, in the content areas such as social studies, English literature, science, Spanish, and some parts of English (where the focus is on comprehension), the students are encouraged to show what they know in a variety of ways and to learn what works best for them. In these courses, what the teacher is looking for is knowledge of the learning outcomes; as long as the student can communicate this knowledge in some way, he or she will be successful in the class.

This approach, known as Show What You Know, can be manifested in many ways by students, from being allowed to draw some or all of the answers on a test, through taking an assessment orally, to having all options open to communicate knowledge. For example, in some classes a student might be able to write the test, make up a test and answer key covering the same content, or show his or her knowledge of the learning outcomes through a video, PowerPoint or Prezi demonstration, song, drama, and/or poem. With teachers who have been using Show What You know for some time, the students no longer need to be told — or taught — the options.

Expanding Our View of Learning

How did we start? Initially the teachers involved were part of a district inquiry group that met consistently over a two-year period. Each teacher collected data on the work their students did when given traditional assignments and when given choice in how they wanted to represent their knowledge. In addition, the teachers kept records of student and parent comments that pertained to the study: some teachers used interviews, others gave surveys to their students, and some kept anecdotal observations. As a group of eight to ten teachers each year, we analyzed more than 500 assignments and assessed each of them using BC Performance Standards.

Since that time, a core group of teachers has continued to do research within their classrooms and collect samples of student work. In addition, this core group of teachers has influenced many staff within their schools, so that more people are now beginning to look at how they too might incorporate some of this thinking into their classrooms.

So what does this thinking do? How does allowing students choice in how they represent their knowledge affect the students and the classrooms? According to the research collected in middle and secondary classrooms over three years, it does quite a number of things:

For Achievement and Engagement

1. It increases the academic achievement of all students and makes learning more meaningful.
   - It helps students focus on learning rather than passing a test.
   - It makes learning deeper as students grapple with content, make connections, and synthesize their understanding.

2. It increases engagement and motivation.
   - It makes learning more interesting and fun.
   - Having choice makes a big difference to all students. Even those students who continue to choose to write an essay say that they feel more a part of the learning/teaching when they get to choose, and are more motivated to do the work.

For the Class

3. It builds relationships between students, and between teachers and students.
   - Students share ideas and often begin working together. As the year progresses they begin to work with other students they might never have chosen to work with before. They see how their interests and talents are similar to someone else's, or they want to learn from someone who has talents very different from their own.
   - The student–teacher relationship changes as the student takes on more ownership of his or her learning. Teachers see aspects of their students that they have never seen before and begin to appreciate new things about the students.

4. It builds classroom community.
    - Students see and recognize other students' strengths.
    - Teachers recognize student strengths and interests. They can show-case student work, expanding the view of success and raising the esteem of more students in the eyes of the rest of the class.

For Student Confidence

5. It builds academic confidence in students, especially in vulnerable students.
    - Many students who rarely pass tests and thought they were "stupid" throughout school begin to see themselves as learners.
    - Many at-risk students are at-risk no longer. They begin to pass courses and gain the confidence they need to take risks in their other courses.

6. It expands students' conception of their own learning.
    - It increases hope for students who have given up at succeeding in school.
    - It increases and encourages creativity in each student and builds new ideas that can be explored in the classroom.
    - It increases traditional writing achievement for some students, as they are more confident that they have something to write about and more willing to take risks.

Although this research has been collected only in middle and secondary classrooms, we have also been using these strategies in elementary class-rooms and university courses.

Starting Points and Starting Small

In a Grade 11 social studies classroom, the teacher told the students that, if they wanted to, they could draw the answer to one of the essay ques-tions instead of writing. He explained that if they were going to draw the answer, they needed to put explanations with each of the drawings so that he wasn't guessing what it was about. He was astounded with the results. Some of the students who never attempted the essays showed that they did know a great deal of the content. They also showed deeper understanding of the concepts through their drawings than they typi-cally did through writing. On the following page is a student response to this essay question: Describe how things changed with the invention of the automobile and other new inventions of the 1920s.

In a Grade 7 classroom, the teacher told the students they could draw or write the plot of the story they had been studying. A young girl with very limited English drew the entire story in a cartoon format. The teacher had had no idea that the student understood so much English, as her speaking and writing were very limited. When the class studied the area of archeology, the student drew a representation of the jobs of an archeologist, and then cut her picture into puzzle pieces. When the

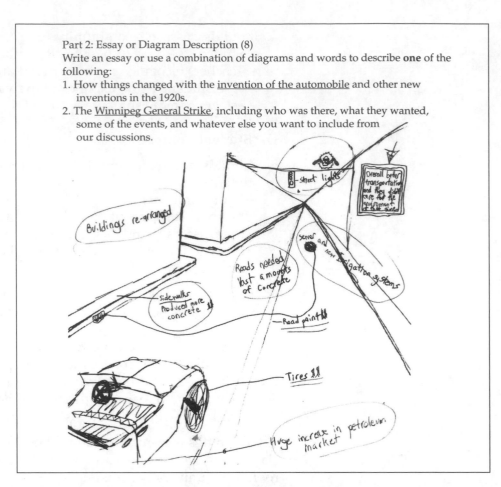

Part 2: Essay or Diagram Description (8)
Write an essay or use a combination of diagrams and words to describe **one** of the following:
1. How things changed with the <u>invention of the automobile</u> and other new inventions in the 1920s.
2. The <u>Winnipeg General Strike</u>, including who was there, what they wanted, some of the events, and whatever else you want to include from our discussions.

teacher questioned her about this, she showed him how it could be put back together and drew parallels between this process and the role of an archeologist, who is continually trying to solve a puzzle. This student with limited English not only understood the content but was making higher-level connections.

In a Grade 3/4 classroom, the teacher consistently gave options for students to draw or write on all comprehension activities, and on any tests or quizzes in social studies and science. It was not only students who had difficulty writing who would choose to draw; many students would use a combination of writing and drawing that showed greater understanding of their knowledge. One of the students always chose to draw, as writing was very difficult for him, but his ideas were huge. Other students wrote, then expanded their ideas through drawing. The sample here shows a Grade 4 student's response to the book *Teammates* by Peter Golenbock. The words answer the questions, but the pictures show a deeper understanding and include emotion and thoughtfulness.

A secondary social studies teacher took the opportunity to have a conversation with one of his students. The student told him that she really knew the information but couldn't write it on the test. She said she never did well on tests. He asked her to tell him what she knew about the particular topic: women's roles in World War Two. She told him all the important facts, and he gave her credit for it.

These are examples of small ways to start. They are also examples of things that have changed students' lives. In each of these cases, students felt inadequate before, and felt adequate afterward. These kinds of choices provide hope to students who may otherwise have very little hope in terms of succeeding in school.

The examples also point out that, in each case, the students knew the answers. The students had the knowledge and had achieved the learning outcomes. They were just not able to communicate their knowledge effectively through writing. The big question is this: What are we assessing? In all content area courses, we need to be assessing student knowledge of the learning outcomes, not the student's ability to write (unless, of course, writing is the learning outcome).

Expanding the Possibilities

When Lev was in Grade 5, his teacher told the class that they were all to make a poster on one type of weather. The teacher explained that the assignment was to include a definition of the type of weather, the location where it happened regularly on earth, the effects, etc. Lev asked the teacher if he could do a movie rather than a poster, and his teacher agreed.

So what did having the choice do for this student? To start with, it made him think creatively. He had to take his topic *blizzards* and show what they were, the damage they did, and where they took place, and think about it in a totally different way. He began his movie by showing himself at the Dairy Queen holding a Blizzard™ frozen treat. He took pictures of toy cars and trucks in a snow bank, making scenes of what the highways looked like during a blizzard; he explored the Internet, watching clips of blizzards, looking at maps, and figuring out how to bring it all together in movie form. He explored the topic in different ways from those he would have had he done a poster.

Now imagine if all students had been given the chance to show their knowledge of the type of weather they chose in whatever way they chose; for example, a talkshow interview with someone who had lived through a tornado, a children's book, a cartoon or song. The teacher creates or co-creates the criteria for success, the elements of content necessary to demonstrate understanding, the learning outcomes that must be covered — but the students decide how they will demonstrate them.

This approach is more creative than traditional learning tasks. It is also more engaging, and the students learn a great deal more. They spend a great deal more energy and time on showing what they know than when they are told to do it one particular way, whether that is an essay, a diorama, or a movie. Very often, if there is no choice, a percentage of kids in the classroom will not be interested in the suggested method, even if the teacher thinks it is fun and engaging. Being open to students' strengths, learning styles, and interests allows us to teach in ways that engage more students.

Three Classrooms, Three Stories

Building Engagement

David Hird teaches Grade 7 in a middle school. He got excited about the idea of Show What You Know several years ago and has never turned back. He says the difference in his teaching now is remarkable. David has always worked hard to create fun and exciting assignments for his students and, because his students liked him, they complied. He has said that what he didn't understand was that some of the students really didn't like the assignments. Since he began to incorporate choice, he has noticed in his students much more enthusiasm about learning, deeper engagement in the tasks, fun in doing classroom work, and a whole new depth of learning.

David describes how surprised he is with the new level of engagement. During an archeological unit, he described to the students six different ways they could show him their understanding of *the role of the archeologist*: write a song, write a poem, write a journal from the point of view of the archeologist, draw a picture that shows the role in detail, write an essay, or conduct an interview. If students had other ideas, David was open to their proposals. What surprised him was that a number of students asked if they could do multiple assignments. David found that, rather than negotiating the assignments down (not wanting to do the whole assignment or trying to make it easier), the students were now negotiating up. They wanted to try them all! David has found that the students are not only engaged in the task, they are putting in more effort and more time because they are enjoying the learning.

Building Community

David Kupec strives to build a student-centred classroom climate that supports, connects, engages, and challenges a diverse body of students. He works to build trust, connectivity, and choice. Without trust, students will not take the risks they need to take to learn. David does many things to build trust in the classroom. He builds strong relationships with each student, and he has found that, when students are given options to represent their learning and begin to be successful, trust and respect grow. Community is built through the connections with him as the teacher and with each other, as they struggle together to support, guide, and develop each other's ideas. David has noticed that learning in this way builds confidence, pride, and a sense of personalized academic hope within each of the students.

In David's classes, both at secondary and middle school, he finds that the Show What You Know practice unites his students: "Students discover the eclectic nature of the classroom population. They see that each one of them can effectively learn, create, and show their knowledge of topical units in individualistic, powerful, and engaging ways." The students begin to see the talents of other students. When this happens, they are drawn to working with students they may never have spent time with previously. Sometimes they choose to work with someone to learn something new from them, other times it's because they have found they have a shared interest. No matter, each time it happens the classroom, community becomes stronger

Building Academic Confidence

Erica Foote teaches English, communications, and social studies in a secondary school. Her communications class is populated with students who feel they are not good at school in general and at English in particular. Erica has worked hard to show these students that they can learn and that many of them learn differently. She uses interesting teaching techniques — including the use of such technology as cell phones, video, and comic-creation tools — to garner their commitment to the class.

What Erica has seen is that success breeds success. As part of the communications class, her students create comics from their reading of *The*

Iliad by Homer. Because they work on this project in groups, she asks them to commit to being there every day so that they don't let their group down. The students dress up in role, take digital pictures of themselves acting out the plot, then add words and create a comic book of the play. The students realize they actually understand a complex play and can easily summarize it for others.

Erica finds that many of these students have talents that simply have not been accessed in their classrooms. The very first time she offered the students a choice in how to summarize a short story they had read, one student, who had never written a word in class, wrote a poem. He met all the criteria and received a higher mark than he had ever received in school. This same student asked her what the next assignment was going to be, as he wanted to get a headstart on it.

In Erica's class, as in other classes that are using students' strengths, teachers are hearing comments that question students' new conceptions of themselves and their learning: "I got an 80! I don't get 80s, I am a 50." "You must be marking easy 'cause I don't get marks like this." As teachers show the students that they have indeed met the criteria of the task, the students start to see that they actually do know the material. It is through these experiences that academic confidence begins to grow. This confidence can also spread to other classes. It is not uncommon for students to ask other teachers in the secondary school questions like "Can I show you what I know in a different way?" "Can I do a rap instead of a paragraph?" "Could I draw the answer instead of writing this essay?" These students are feeling empowered. They are beginning to understand their own personal strengths, and they know that they should not always have to use writing to communicate their knowledge.

Assessment

So how does this work when it comes to assessment? Many teachers question the idea of assessing creative projects. The answer is that they are not assessing the creativity; they are assessing whether or not the learning outcomes are met. Has the student shown his or her knowledge for the learning outcomes that the teacher is assessing? At what depth?

Using strategies from Assessment For Learning (AFL), the teacher outlines the learning outcomes being covered in any particular unit of study, and then lets the students know which learning outcomes need to be covered specifically in each assignment. The teacher also provides an assessment rubric so that there are no surprises for the student.

Some teachers build the rubrics with their students to make them more meaningful; some create rubrics and give them to their students. Most teachers have some exemplars of what other students have done to show their knowledge, both to stimulate ideas and to show that the learning outcomes must be met for the student to do well. Showing stronger and weaker exemplars also gives the teacher a chance to talk about how some assignments handed in might be creative, or beautifully done, but do not necessarily meet the learning outcomes. Students begin to understand that representing their learning in various forms is just as rigorous as writing, but can be more interesting and engaging, and has the potential to provide deeper learning. In all classrooms where choice is offered, teachers have found that, compared to traditional tasks, creative-choice tasks elicit more effort from students, and their learning is deeper as they struggle to communicate in different ways.

Opening Up Traditional Assessments

As teachers, we have a choice in how we assess student learning. Is it more time-consuming to grade assignments and projects than to mark a multiple-choice test? Absolutely. Multiple-choice tests give a very narrow picture of what a student knows. Students are required only to match a teacher's thinking, not to present their own thinking, when generating a response. These tests reflect who is good at memorizing information rather than who has a deep understanding or the ability to synthesize and apply information. Multiple-choice tests do not reflect the skills required of 21st-century learners.

The standard test in many secondary schools is a combination of multiple-choice, short-answer, and essay questions. For students who don't do well with multiple-choice questions, or who have difficulty with writing, these tests can be very discouraging. Again, they are limiting, both for the teacher in terms of understanding what the student knows, and for the student in terms of showing what they know.

Any product/demonstration should both show what students know and further develop what they know. In transforming/personalizing their learning (Learning Stage 3 of strategies to enhance learning; see page 44 in chapter 4), students deepen their understanding. For some students, the essay form helps them synthesize their learning, and transform and personalize the content. For others, the form limits them. A wider assortment of options enables a wider range of students to demonstrate their learning. We believe in inclusive classrooms that honor and support all students; expanding our view of how we can represent knowledge enhances success for more learners.

We are in the business of learning. If we are serious about finding out what students know, then we have to be willing to think more expansively and more flexibly. Sometimes teachers feel they are "cheating" or "going easy on a student" if they let a student do an exam orally or draw instead of write. We have become so convinced that writing is the purest form of communicating knowledge that we see other forms as easier or less meaningful, when, in fact, they help many students make connections and think more deeply.

Students need mentors: people who see things inside them that they may not see themselves, or people who believe in them and can pull out the best in them (Robinson, 2001). Many students do not know what strengths they have unless someone helps them see these strengths or provides opportunities for them to experience them. We have that opportunity in our classrooms — a chance to help all our students gain academic confidence by acknowledging the strengths that they bring to learning and by developing new strengths.

6

Building an Inclusive Culture in a Secondary Classroom

authored by
NARYN SEARCY

For a number of reasons, the focus on belonging and inclusion loses its momentum in most high-school classrooms. A teacher could argue any number of reasons for its absence, including a demanding curriculum, lack of class time, intense pressure to have students perform on provincial exams, increased maturity of the students, and expectations for independent work over group collaboration. When a high-school class focuses mainly on the coverage of curriculum and students rarely speak to each other, what need is there to build inclusion or community?

We believe in an expanded goal — to create a community where the teacher and the students participate in and contribute to the learning of the group and where students demonstrate their understanding in a variety of ways. This goal requires an explicit focus on community, and inclusion is essential. Even in a rigorous academic course, where curricular demands constantly compete with limited class time, a targeted focus on collaboration and team-building pays dividends. Not only do students feel better about coming to class and participating in the learning, they also learn more. But this increase in commitment does involve a shift in focus. Instead of thinking of the purpose of the class as being to get the curriculum across to the students, the teacher must focus on what the experience of the class will be for the students and how learning the curriculum can take place within that community.

Almost anyone who has ever coached a team or sponsored an extra-curricular activity will attest to the importance it brings to a student's overall school experience. Extra-curricular activities allow us to see different strengths in students, and allow students to build confidence and connect with other students. Many teachers would agree that extra-curricular activities are sometimes the only thing that connects some of our at-risk students to the school. But does it have to be this way? School coaches, drama club directors, and art club sponsors are among those staff acutely aware of the need to connect students with their passions and to create a sense of team and self-worth. Can we not make these kinds of connections within the classroom, using student passion and a sense of team to support student learning? In other words, why can't we run our classrooms the way we coach a team? One of the obvious arguments against this perspective is that, unlike mandatory attendance in class, participation in a sport or club is optional and students volunteer for it. They choose to be there. However, the advantage the classroom teacher has is that, in a class, everyone can get playing time! No one has to be the star. The students do not have to compete with one another; they can truly collaborate.

In this chapter, Naryn Searcy, a secondary classroom teacher, explains how she uses ideas of inclusion and community to build a team in her classroom. Her examples are from Literature 12, but she uses the same principles in her English 9 and English 11 classrooms. This chapter is Naryn's story.

Building a Community

As I sit here writing to you, Sam is rushing around the house trying to get out the door in time for your class. I'm well aware that he doesn't have the best track record at school for a variety of reasons. You cannot believe how good it is to see him excited to go to school for the first time since he was in elementary school. Through the years, if he talks about school at all, it has negative connotations. He talks about your class regularly and in a very excited, positive way. Thank you for igniting a spark in my son.

— Parent e-mail

In our classroom the emphasis is on working together and supporting each other. Students are told from the first day that this class may be taught differently from other classes they have experienced. First of all, students need to get used to the idea that they do not exist only as individuals. In this class, they are responsible for themselves and for others as well. If one person does not show up for class, then they are missed. If twenty-nine students are present and one is missing, then the class is incomplete. The students begin to understand that their presence or absence affects everyone in the classroom, and that if someone fails or succeeds it says something about them as a group.

I tell the students a story I learned in Grade 8 from my basketball coach. My coach told the team that when we walked in the gym for practice we had to take off our *jackets*. Whoever the team members were considered to be outside the gym — whether it be jocks, geeks, or smokers — that label had to come off when we walked through the door. Once in the gym, we were all members of the team working toward a common goal. This same concept applies when my students walk into my literature classroom. The labels have to come off. This can be a difficult task for students who have seen themselves (and others) occupying a certain role or having a certain relationship with others for the past twelve years. However, it is a "non-negotiable" of the classroom. Once in the door, students are all just *lit students* working toward a common goal of making the class experience as memorable and as meaningful as possible.

Students choose a *lit name* for themselves. This is the name they will be called throughout the course. It is even used on their report cards. Some examples from recent classes include *Samurai* for a student named Sam, *Graham Cracka* for Graham, *White Lightning*, *Sir Pintata II*, *The Guru's Assistant*, and *Recyclops*. The taking of a lit name is another step toward separating students from any previous history or cliques outside the classroom. It allows for fun and individuality, but also creates an identity that is recognized and accepted within the community of the class.

A few weeks into the course, as our comfort and confidence with each other has grown, I share a movie clip from *Backdraft* with the students. In the *Backdraft* clip, two firefighters are caught in a burning building when a huge explosion occurs. The two men tumble off a ledge; one manages to desperately hang on with one arm while holding the second, who dangles below him. If either falls, certain death awaits him. It is immediately evident that the firefighter holding on to the ledge cannot possibly lift both the other man and himself back to safety, so the man hanging on to him says, "Let me go," and releases his grip. The first man looks down, refusing to let go, and says, "If you go, we go."

The message in the clip is clear. One man does not exist without the other. They both survive or they both die. It is the ultimate example of "team." After showing the clip, I ask the students to apply this lesson to our literature class. We discuss what kind of culture is possible in our classroom, and I tell them they can be part of something special if they are willing to commit to something bigger than themselves. For many students, this may be one of their first experiences of learning in a real community, where knowledge is shared and understood together and where helping each other is encouraged.

Building Confidence and Taking Risks

Building community does not happen just by talking about it. It involves teaching students how to encourage and support others in their learning and in their risk-taking. In my classroom, I want to see students expressing themselves using their strengths and having no fear of ridicule or embarrassment. We start small.

I want the students to be comfortable speaking, acting, drawing, or even singing in front of their peers. I have found that simply offering students creative options for expressing their knowledge is no guarantee that students will try one of them. First, students have to feel valued and necessary. Secondly, they must be comfortable taking risks. Finally, students must be exposed to the powerful learning that can happen when they use their strengths (speaking, drama, art, writing) to show their understanding, and be given lots of time to practice and play with the different options. Students are exposed to various options for expression (artistic, verbal, kinesthetic) from a very early point in the course. They are given explicit instructions on how to complete some options, and they are often given examples from previous classes. A *gradual release* model is used, wherein students initially take risks with a partner or group and then later try independently.

I talk to my students about taking small risks. I explicitly tell them where I expect them to be in relation to their comfort zone. I use the chart on page 63 to explain that we all have a comfort zone; I tell them that people who exist only within that zone never discover what they are truly capable of, because they play it safe. On the other hand, students who are pushed too far outside their comfort zone shut down, because the risk is simply too great and the possibility of success does not outweigh the fear of failure. I tell the students that my job is to keep them just outside their comfort zone on a regular basis. Students have to be willing to take risks, even if it means some failure. I want them to begin to experience the understanding that failure is learning in itself and that it must be possible in our classroom.

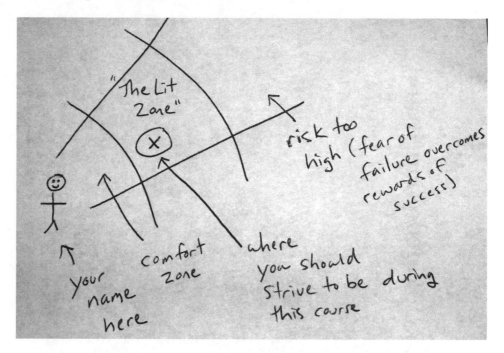

From then on, in our classroom, students are given opportunities to take small risks on a regular basis. It might be as small as standing on a desk, holding a soft sword in their hands, or reading one line of poetry aloud. The whole class practices giving huge ovations for anyone willing to take the smallest risks. All performances in class are expected to be greeted with enthusiastic applause.

I believe that one of the reasons so many students are willing to take risks is because it is never *required*. I am expecting them to take risks, but am not demanding a risk-taking experience at a certain time, on a certain day. Students are always given opportunities to share their views and are encouraged to stand up and read aloud, but they always know they may choose not to. Indeed, the rare student goes through the course without ever standing up and presenting, but that is the students' choice and they must have that safety net. Even the most boisterous and outgoing student needs the option of not having to perform on any given day.

Smaller activities lead to bigger ones. Getting up and reading one line of poetry builds confidence for larger passages, then possibly skits or plays or songs. Early in the course, students are given many opportunities to draw, act, or orally report their understanding of what they have learned in class. For students who are more reticent to participate, there are ways to help them feel more comfortable:

- *Group Work:* All students are given the option to act or present in groups. There is a feeling of safety when someone else is up there with you.

- *Costumes*: Dressing up not only is fun, but it also allows some students to feel more comfortable presenting in front of others, as the costume provides some separation between the audience and the student.

- *Puppet shows*: Puppet theatre is an excellent transition for students who may be shy, who are able to speak out loud but may not want to be directly visible to the audience.

- *Video*: If students have the ability to use video, they can present material orally (and bring in other options) without the fear of standing up directly in front of the class.

- *Non-speaking Roles*: This option works for many students who are terrified to use their voices. For these students, participation in a skit or play could be in a non-speaking role, such as holding up a sign or taking the place of scenery.

For the first few weeks in class, a culture of appreciation for risk-taking is established, as is the knowledge that students step outside their comfort zone only of their own accord. If they choose never to speak out and want to respond only in writing, then that is their choice.

Assessment: Practice without Penalty

Early in the course, students are given many opportunities to practice demonstrating their understanding in different ways without having to worry about marks. They have read poetry aloud, created a group podcast, created and presented group posters, and acted out skits for descriptive feedback — not for marks. Students have numerous opportunities to show their understanding in different ways, and are offered many invitations to take chances in front of their peers and be acknowledged. These opportunities allow the students to think about the content of the course more creatively and to practice different ways of representing their knowledge individually and in groups before doing an independent project that will be evaluated.

Below are some sample activities from a lesson on the poem "To A Mouse" by Robert Burns. This lesson carries over a two-day period. Students study the poem as a class and then are asked to represent their knowledge of the poem in a variety of ways. The students understand that they are doing this to learn, they will not be receiving marks on this assignment. This is an example of *practice without penalty*.

- Students are introduced to the poet Robert Burns and his poem "Auld Lang Syne." To make connections, I lead the class through a team connecting activity where the students work in pairs to discuss a positive memory they have. I reinforce the value of friendships and relationships that are formed over time and remind students that this course is always meant to link to reality.

- Students are then given a copy of "To A Mouse," a poem written in a very difficult traditional Scottish dialect. Students are given the opportunity to read a stanza aloud. This is a very difficult poem to read, but a very safe one, because no one in the class knows what the words are really supposed to sound like. Loud cheering follows every reading. Students stand on their desks to read the words (the rest of the class might decide they want to stand on their desks too, in support).

- Students are divided into partners and each group of two is given a stanza to decipher. Partners read their ideas aloud to the rest of the class, and I fill any gaps in meaning or clarify any misinterpretation of language. I make sure to reinforce student understanding of the two key themes in the poem: *mankind has broken its union with nature*, and *even our best laid plans often do not work out.*

- For five minutes I teach the concept of *microcosm* and explain how the seemingly insignificant event described in "To a Mouse" actually demonstrates universal truths. The class discusses examples of various things the poem could represent in the real world. They decide that the mouse could represent the poor and oppressed, while the farmer symbolizes the wealthy and powerful. The mouse might represent the natural world, while the farmer embodies destructive forces, such as pollution or global warming.

- Students are asked to show their understanding of the poem and the key themes, and are given some different options for how they might like to do this.

Option 1
They may do a Mouse Dance. All eight stanzas of the poem, as well as a specific reference to the two key themes of the poem, must be re-enacted. Students have a choice of performing the dance to "Do You Think I'm Sexy" by Rod Stewart, "500 Miles" by the Proclaimers, or "Saturday Night" by the Bay City Rollers — all songs by Scottish bands. Students can work in groups of up to four.

Option 2
Students may represent the eight stanzas of the poem and the two key themes in a comic format that combines drawings with brief written explanations. Students are provided with a blank comic-strip template. Students can do this individually or with a partner.

Option 3
Students may do *reduced poetry*. For this option, students take each of the eight stanzas and the two key themes and reduce each of them to only four words. For example, the stanza that includes the key theme "The best laid plans of mice and men often go awry" could be reduced to "good plans often fail." Students can do this individually or in partners.

This assignment always works! I believe it is because the stage has been set and students are now ready and able to work with choice. They have three distinctly different ways of presenting their understanding of the poem. In each case the criteria is the same:

- demonstrate understanding of the meaning of each of the eight stanzas of the poem
- recognize and demonstrate the two key themes

As the students work on their projects, I circulate around the class and give feedback. The dance groups hand in a brief written explanation of what each part of their dance means or give a verbal explanation in front of the class after the dance has been performed. I respond to the comic and poetry assignments after class. In each case, if a stanza has been incorrectly interpreted or a theme has been missed, I give feedback. I use three questions — What worked? What's missing? What's next? — to frame my thinking as I give feedback based on the criteria.

This activity is not a long one; usually all of the groups have completed their work within thirty minutes. The final results do not need to be polished. At the end of the lesson, students have worked to understand the poem; they have had the opportunity to engage with other members of the class; they have worked with criteria; and they have had the chance to work with the material in a way that suits their interests and talents (kinesthetic, artistic, written). Students are focused and on-task, not because they are being evaluated or watched for on-task behavior, but because they are working on a project that suits the elements of expression they are most comfortable with. Despite the speed of the activity and the fact that there are no official marks, the results are of good quality. Students put effort into activities they enjoy.

As the course continues and the positive culture continues to build, I find that students take more and more risks. A number of things happen. Students begin to show their interests, talents, and strengths to others: they sing, dance, act, draw, build, rap, or write to express themselves. As they do this, the community becomes richer and also more inclusive. Many students have strengths and talents that we never see in our classrooms because there is no place for them to show them. In our classroom, students are taking notice of other's strengths, learning things about each other that they never knew before, encouraging and supporting each other, and learning to respect each other in new ways. They are engaged. The academic interest and depth of understanding of English literature increases — I believe because the students are connecting it to their lives and working together in a learning community.

Diverse Students, Improved Performance

Student Achievement

While one focus of the class is inclusion and community, there is always the overarching reality that Literature 12 is a provincially examinable course with a rigorous curriculum and challenging content. While the provincial exam is now optional and only a minority of students write it, for the first three years I taught the course the exam was mandatory. My students have always done well on the provincial exam and my approach to the class was no different when the exam was required.

Students who write the exam are successful and their results are always above the provincial average. My participation rates for the exam are significantly higher than the rest of the province. In my current classes, whether a student opts to write the provincial exam or not, I cover all of the prescribed learning outcomes.

Class Composition

Despite the traditional reputation of Literature 12 as an elite course composed of strong writers and passionate readers, at my school the course includes students from every background, including those considered to be at risk academically, behaviorally, or socially. It is not uncommon to have students in Lit 12 from the Alternate Education Program, or those who take Communications 12 (a course offered in BC for students who would have difficulty completing English 12 in order to graduate). While the course still attracts strong academic students, it has a reputation as a class in which any student can be successful. I am very proud of the school-wide belief that "every kid is a potential Lit kid." The students in Lit 12 are achieving academically, socially, and personally. A community of learners is developing, even in this last year of high school.

7

Building an Inclusive Culture in an Intermediate Classroom

authored by

KIM ONDRIK

"People are like trees, and groups of people are like the forests.
While the forests are composed of many different kinds of trees,
these trees intertwine their roots so strongly that it is impossible for the strongest winds which blow on our islands to uproot the forest,
for each tree strengthens its neighbor, and their roots are inextricably intertwined.
In the same way the people of our Islands,
composed of members of Nations and races from all over the world,
are beginning to intertwine their roots so strongly that no troubles will affect them.
Just as one tree standing alone would soon be destroyed by the first strong wind which came along,
so it is impossible for any person, any family, or any community to stand alone against the troubles of this world."

— Chief Skidegate, Lewis Collinson, March 1966

There are many ways to build an inclusive classroom, a classroom where all learners feel safe and where all learners are engaged in learning. So far in this book: in chapter 4, teaching with the end in mind and strategic teaching are presented as the structures that support learning for all students; in chapters 5 and 6, choice is a key element. Another approach that is gaining credibility among teachers is project-based learning.

In project-based learning, student learning is guided by an overarching question or problem. These are real-world questions and problems, those that engage students in authentic exploration and in-depth study. Because students are searching for real answers to real questions and are expected to share their results with real audiences, the learning tends to be highly motivational, personal, and deeply engaging. Students lead the learning while teachers work as guides on the side, coaching, advising, supporting, and encouraging. That we adapt to meet the needs of individual students is a given. Most projects extend over a significant time period and are often collaborative.

In-depth learning is one critical aspect of project-based learning, but of equal importance is the collaborative, team-based nature of the exploration. Student relationships are strengthened as students work together, whether exploring team questions or individual ones. The classroom truly becomes a learning community, where all participants are engaged in powerful learning, supporting one another in their search for answers. The teachers' role is to build and maintain the environment that allows this to happen. Kim Schonert-Reichl calls this pedagogical caring. Her research clearly supports the critical nature of working together to create caring and supportive environments that foster belonging and school success for all students. As students enter the intermediate grades and middle school, more is expected of them academically and they tend to feel less sense of belonging. Connectedness matters. It makes a difference in learning. (Schonert-Reichl, 2008)

A supportive and caring environment is important to Kim Ondrik, a Grade 6/7 teacher. She strives to have all her students become resilient, caring, competent, independent, and interdependent people. Learning in

Kim's class unfolds as projects. It is messy. It is exciting. It is involving. It includes and enhances all learners. This chapter is Kim's story.

Growing a Community

Our classroom, called the *O-zone*, is an animated, organic, and naturally messy Grade 6/7 forest of interconnected learners. The variety of trees is staggering and quite beautiful. Some have been well-nourished; their roots go deep and reach from home to school; they stand majestic and tall. Others find they must uproot at the end of each school day and then re-root each morning; long weekends and holidays restrict their growth in significant ways. These trees have not yet reached the maturity they were made for and long for. Some live in rich humus that stimulates continuous growth. Some haven't enjoyed the warmth of the sun in a while, and it's difficult to thrive when others have grown taller and blocked the sky from view. Some have adapted to their environments, finding strategies that support growth. Some have branches that are numerous, but roots that are few — the slightest wind that comes uproots them and turns them upside-down. The trees vary widely in growth.

When visitors step into our forest, they usually comment on the collection of words, images, and artifacts we have hanging all over the classroom. We explain that the O-zone is a community and, like any community, it needs these things to help tell our story. It's a scrapbook of sorts: each object or idea is deeply rooted in experiences the O-zone has engaged in over the last five years. Visitors wonder why we would want to recycle memories. As a teacher, I may find the clutter unbearable at times, but honoring a culture and nurturing a developing forest is messy roll-up-your-sleeves business. What I know for sure is that, like trees, children need warmth and connection in order to grow.

In the past five years, I have learned that people talk about building a community as if it's home construction: the contractor (teacher) receives plans from an architect (professional development sources) and then begins clearing the land, laying the foundation — as if community-building is a linear and controllable process. I have found that, instead of home construction, it is the organic metaphor of the forest that more accurately describes the process and the deeper purposes of community-building in a classroom. If the goal of education is to promote growth and learning in each and every learner, then seeing each child as a unique plant requiring particular growing conditions is a critical (and challenging) belief to hold dear. What is common in each learner, however, is that focusing upon his or her deep root growth (rather than superficial understanding) will help to produce the kinds of obvious fruits of confidence, success, and lifelong learning!

So, in the O-zone, we (students and teachers with the support of parents, teaching assistants, and administrators) have established expectations. These seem to stimulate deep root growth as well as promoting emotional safety for the tender saplings. They are revisited and re-presented each fall as the new Grade 6 students join the old ones (the

"If adults provide tasks for children that are perceived to be interesting and worthwhile and they believe that they can accomplish, children are more likely to develop a sense of their competency. If they are not provided with opportunities to learn skills in supportive and caring contexts, they can then develop a sense of inferiority and incompetence."

— Kim Schonert-Reichl

"I've noticed that when classes are communities, if a student (or the teacher) is stuck and having a hard time coping, we have each other to lean on and get us out of the 'mud.' Like when my friend had his iPod stolen, our whole class had a talking circle meeting and we all pitched in and helped buy him a new iPod, or when we proved other adults wrong when we showed that a student with autism can become an excellent problem-solver and can do everything we can do without a CEA's support. As a community we can accomplish anything because we're stronger together than we are apart."

— Charis, age 12

69

present Grade 7 students) and have always been found to be meaningful. Frankly, they just make sense to the kids, and I constantly refer to them in our day-to-day interactions.

Expectations of the O-zone Community

1. Community first, individual second.
2. Fairness isn't sameness.
3. We need to voice problems as they happen.
4. Talking circles are the way we solve problems.
5. We all learn in different ways.
6. We need to be presented information in different ways.
7. We need to show what we know in different ways.
8. We need to celebrate!
9. We can eat healthy food whenever we need to.
10. We can leave if frustrated.

"The community feel of our class lets me be relaxed and I don't like being in a tense classroom. I think when I'm relaxed I grow and learn way better. In a community-first class you can trust everyone. In an individual-first class you basically only trust your teacher. When you trust everyone, it makes things a lot easier. We are all teachers in our class."

—Anthony, age 12

In September, I focus the children on us, the O-zone. We explore what expectations mean and the value of community in the learning and growing of individuals. We discuss what a democratic classroom looks like: How does the role of an authority figure fit? What do I do if I am a minority voice? We uncover who we are as individuals: strengths, talents, personality, quirks, natural roles, areas of special or unique needs, the variety of individual experiences. We learn how to problem-solve using a model of restorative justice: accepting there is a problem; owning your part of the problem; hearing the others' points of view; understanding the roots of the issue; apologizing from your heart and forgiving (being willing to "blow the problem away" and not bring it up again). In October we start to move beyond building relationships and serving the community: mentoring with our buddy classes; exploring the wetland habitat behind our school; leading community events like Rivers Day; and volunteering at the food bank.

A Project-Learning Approach

The most effective way I have found (so far) to uphold the expectations, build upon our values, and reawaken the natural curiosity in learning in these "tweenagers" has been to focus on project learning. Of course, there are many lessons I prepare and offer to the students throughout the week that infuse meaning and deepen their understanding of a variety of learning processes and content. These intertwine with the projects in progress or provide the stimulus from which new projects emerge. From time to time, I give formative or summative assessments that push me past my perceptions of where individuals are at any given time. These inform my interactions with learners, and provide data for end-of-term reports to parents as well.

In project learning, students explore real-world issues, challenges, and questions, while at the same time developing cross-curriculum skills as they work in small collaborative groups and sometimes independently.

Projects inspire students to be actively engaged in their learning. The public presentation at the end of the process creates accountability and positive stress. The questions, comments, feedback, and concerns requested after each presentation create a purpose and reason to put in a strong effort. Consequently, students tend to understand the themes, concepts, or ideas in a deep way. A student named Justine once told me, "I have grown into a community girl by getting feedback and accepting it. Accepting it helps me understand and that helps me be a better person. Embrace feedback and care about it, accept it. Don't push it away." All students are active participants in learning. On page 72 is an overview of The O-Zone Process for Creating Powerful Projects that is posted in our classroom.

As the process unwinds, I use a checklist of learning outcomes across the curriculum to monitor what is being explored. I then teach those outcomes necessary to enhance or deepen understanding for the learners. This is sometimes done through individual consultation, peer mentoring, or whole-class instruction. I must discern what would work best for *this* particular group of students. I have found that there is no procedure that works best for everyone all the time.

An Example of Project Learning in the Classroom

Day One

Today, the forest of faces looks confused and slightly shaken.

"What do you mean that most of us are immigrants, Mrs. O?"

"Yeah, I was born at Vernon Jubilee Hospital."

"Me too! That just doesn't make any sense."

"Well, yes, unless you have Aboriginal ancestors, your family was originally from somewhere else in the world," I explain, enjoying the confusion and questioning. Something powerful is happening.

There is silence as the students ruminate on the message. Then Noah's quiet voice, full of conviction, breaks the calm. "I propose we do a project on our family trees so we can find out where we're from." Many eyes glance at me. I smile and nod.

Noah stands. "All in favor? Great, it's a majority!"

Although it's only September, the O-zone's "looping" philosophy has half the class returning for their Grade 7 year. Projects from previous years are displayed all over the walls, propped on all available shelving, as well as hanging from the ceiling tiles. This stimulates lively conversation on the first day of school as the "veterans" explain the process of creating a project with the "rookies." I am always in awe of the language of these second-year students — they have become extremely metacognitive and sound very adult. They are superb models for our new students.

"Projects help me learn because they are engaging," Levi volunteers. "Doing projects is more interesting than worksheets. With worksheets, you're not being creative and expressing yourself. Worksheets have always shut me down."

The O-Zone Process for Creating Powerful Projects

BEGINNING

How can I best be successful?
- work alone?
- with a partner?
- in a group?
- assign roles based upon strengths

Begin with the end in mind:
- an outcome demonstrated
- a deep question answered
- a challenge met

Study the expectations & rubric

RESEARCH

What are the possible sources?
- books, newspapers & magazines (libraries: class, school, community)
- internet
- films
- interviews
- conversations

Have I explored at least 3 points of view?
- importance of triangulation

(HOW IS THE RESEARCH SHARED AMONGST GROUP MEMBERS?)

ORGANIZE

What are the most effective methods?
- cut & paste
- in a binder or journal
- lists
- webs/clusters
- word documents
- save on the server/flash drive

Guiding Questions:
- 3 points of view?
- 3 sources for each?
- on track with rubric?

(HOW CAN THE GROUP STAY ORGANIZED & SHARE THE WORK?)

PROJECT DESIGN

What kinds of projects could I/we use?

Should I/we try something new?

What has been effective for me or others in the past?

Who will the audience be?

What will most engage the audience?

POLISH

Proofread & edit

Feedback:
- from at least 3 peers
- from one adult

Respond to the feedback:
- does it make sense?
- what part should I/we use?
- what part should I/we ignore?

Compare project to the rubric

Prepare for presentation
(EQUALLY SHARE "AIR TIME" AMONGST GROUP MEMBERS)

PRESENT

Day before:
- do we have everything I need?

Night before:
- get a good night rest

Day of:
- get presentation ready
- talk to partners
- briefly rehearse

Who is invited to view presentations?

Who will assess the presentations?

After the presentation:
QUESTIONS, COMMENTS, FEEDBACK, CONCERNS?

CELEBRATE

Cake?

Pembroke Publishers © 2011 *Learning in Safe Schools, revised edition* by Faye Brownlie and Judith King ISBN 978-1-55138-266-1

"I think projects help kids a lot in learning because they give them a time to learn and be creative," states Brianna with confidence.

"Yeah," enthuses Cassy. "Projects are great for us kids to have a say in what we like and do. They have helped me in exploring different perspectives in life because it's not just researching for information. We get to listen to other people talk about their projects. This makes me think and gives me deep memories."

"Well," says Brianna, "I think projects help me learn better than worksheets because with projects you're getting your hands into the information and fishing out the good stuff — sort of like with cranberries!"

There are some nods, some smiles, and some questioning looks from the students new to the process.

Sensing some confusion, Brianna continues. "Projects also give you the opportunity to work with other people and not just fill in the blanks and not really think for yourself. Also projects are really good for learning how to present ideas!"

"Well, project learning helps me with my learning because learning with other people helps me learn more," reflects Alexis. "On any project that we're doing, there isn't just one opinion. It has as many people's opinions as are in your group. You can see that too during presentations because, by listening to others' projects, you are basically piggy-backing on their research and learning."

And so our geneology project begins. The students hungrily dive into Internet search, seeking answers to the deep question of "Where did I come from?" I don't interfere. No tight reins today. The energy in the classroom is palpable. I have learned that I can use this time, when the students are thoroughly engaged, to observe individual work habits and social interaction, and to ask probing questions about the way each student is approaching his or her learning. These moments of self-direction are a gift. I can serve and challenge every unique learner only as I come to know him or her well. As the process continues, much time is eaten up in helping struggling learners, facilitating deeper understandings, supporting the students in discovering materials for their presentations, and, for some, finding quiet places to work somewhere in the school.

"I'll see you later, Mrs. O," says Matthew. "It's just too noisy in here. I can't think!" I nod my head in agreement and suggest he look at the agenda to determine when he needs to return.

Day Two

I remind the students of the O-zone project structure (page 72) and the particular expectations we have worked up for this family tree project (page 74). We have the process posted on the whiteboard with magnetic names so the students can move themselves along as they journey toward the presentation deadline. With this particular project we agree that it's best to work individually. After all, no two of us have exactly the same ancestry.

We discuss the established criteria for project work and examine how we will be judged so we remember and can to refer to the expectations as we actively engage in the exploration.

Where have I come from?

We have all ended up in Vernon *for a variety of reasons.*

This challenge will help us to *dig deeper* **& learn where we are** *rooted in history.*

September 2010

Genealogy

(from Greek: γενεά, genea, "generation"; and λόγος, logos, "knowledge")

is the study of families and the tracing of their lineages and history. Genealogists use oral traditions, historical records, genetic analysis, and other records to obtain information about a family. The results are displayed in many different ways: models, drawings, books, posters, movies, keynotes, speeches, etc.

EACH PROJECT SHOULD DEMONSTRATE *as complete* **A FAMILY HISTORY** *as possible.*

The Ozone *Process* of Creating an *Excellent* Project

Beginning	Research	Organize	Project Design	Polish	Present	Celebrate
- Work alone ? With a partner ? Group ? - Begin with the end in mind: • an outcome demonstrated • a deep question answered • a challenge - Study rubric	- Have I explored at least 3 points of view ? - Triangulation ... - Sources: • Books - class, school, community libraries • Technology • Interviews • Conversations	- Methods: • cut & paste • in a binder • lists • webs/clusters • word documents - Questions: • 3 points of view ? • 3 sources for each ? • on track with rubric ?	- What kinds of projects could I use ? - Should I try something new ? - What has worked for me or others in the past ?	- ask for feedback from 3 peers - respond to the feedback - proofread, edit - compare project to rubric - rehearse - prepare for presentation	- day before: do I have everything I need ? - night before: get a good rest - day of: get presentation ready, rehearse, talk to partnerm stay calm	

proposed by Noah Lee ~ Created by Kim Ondrik

1

74

Nick, in Grade 7, asks if he can work with a partner. "I feel more successful in a team," he says.

"I don't think that will work for this project, Nick," I reply. "This is a very personal project. It's about *your* ancestors. I'm comfortable, though, with you seeking feedback from others as you work on your project. What do you think?"

"Yeah, I guess so. It's hard, though!" He stomps his foot and turns to find his laptop in the cart.

I smile and acknowledge the challenge of exploring a question; the challenge of standing in front of your peers and presenting what you were able to discover, sometimes tiny, sometimes huge, but always your own; tolerating the vulnerability you feel when receiving feedback about what you were able to create and present. Projects provide freedom, but at the same time require a personal responsibility that Nick knows from experience to be difficult.

Ongoing Research and Feedback

"I have grown so much in this class. For example, I have been feeling awkward in this class because I wasn't used to it. But now, this learning that I *thought* was pointless, will help me with individuals all through my life!"

— Madison, age 11

Anticipating the first project presentations of the year (usually at the end of October or beginning of November) creates tension and anxiety in the O-zone. By the time each turn arrives, however, the peer audience listens deeply, findings are expressed and seeds of confidence are planted. Asking for "questions, comments, feedback, concerns" allows peers to appreciate each other's personal voice and unique perspective: "I really like that you tried and didn't give up. Even though you weren't prepared, you were brave to try."

The exploration prompts new questions and connections. The students are intrigued:

> "Hey, there are Quibells in Quebec. I wonder if my ancestors were French?"

> "Hey, I found a Russian Commander with the same last name as me. Do you think we're related? Now this is COOL!"

About a week into the research, I invite a guest geneologist, Leanne Botterill, to visit and share her vocation with the children. She shows the students how she discovered her ancestry and includes copies of official documentation for them to peruse. It's a challenge and requires magnifying glasses.

> "Wow, look how tiny and strange the printing is. I can barely read it!"

> "What's a census, Leanne?"

I follow Leanne's lead and bring my own family's documentation into the classroom for the students to look at: report cards, birth and death certificates, journals. Some pieces are formal and others, more casual. All, however, tell a story. Wesley brings in a family tree that a relative has created, beautifully presented on parchment. His great-grandfather was a founding member of Vancouver's Chinatown. It makes Wesley feel important. His peers celebrate! Wesley is assembling pieces of where he has come from. His roots grow deeper. This research is helping him make sense of his life. For the first time in his life, he is proud to be of Chinese descent.

Pat, the beloved Classroom Educational Assistant (CEA) of the O-zone, brings in boxes of very old family photographs and piles of old documents. She is her family's memory keeper. Pat decides to create her own project on where she has come from. There are many stories to tell, and some bring tears to her eyes. She inspires the children with her focus and passion. They come to her with questions.

This project brings to light the tragedy of residential schools for Aboriginal families. Several children cannot find any information about their native ancestry. There is disappointment expressed.

> "This doesn't make any sense. We were here on Turtle Island before the European people."

The Internet frustrates these students, and the loss of culture and identity that many Aboriginal families experienced after contact leave them with very few stories to tell. I seize the opportunity to teach some Canadian history lessons. Questions are raised. Roots go deeper as they explore this injustice. I make a mental note to ensure further exploration in another project — *Rabbit-Proof Fence* (Miramax, 2002) would be an amazing film to explore in this respect.

Preparing Presentations

After weeks of research, both at school and at home with parents, grandparents, aunts, and uncles, the students are full of ideas and excitement. Each starts to organize his information and creates a vision for the very best way to "show what he/she knows" in a presentation. This is a creative and messy season. The more precise and conservative students find this part disconcerting. The more self-directed and creative students love it!

> "What do you mean I have to show **and** tell?"

> "What do you mean I have to try to engage four senses?"

> "I don't think I'll use a keynote. Remember last year how too many people used it and it became boring?"

> "Do we have any plasticine? I love to build. I think I'll actually make a tree!"

> "Could I make a tree cake, Mrs. O? I know how engaged I am as a listener when I get to have something to eat after the presentation."

From time to time, I pause the activity and remind the students of the process. We reflect on where we are and where we are going next. We discuss what's going well and any frustrations that have arisen. I continue to ask questions and get the students to think more about what exactly they are asking or thinking about. I get them to explain their thinking and use "tell me more" questions to get them to go deeper. The learning is powerful, and implicit thinking is made explicit for all to wrestle with.

I have designed a log where I can make note of each student's journey. At report card time, this is very valuable!

Presentation day is anticipated as the week begins. Friday is only five days away, so polishing the presentations needs to become the focus. Students begin to notice where others are in the process. For some, panic sets in.

Austin comes to me: "I'm not ready yet, Mrs. O. I don't know what to do. I won't be ready on Friday."

"Sorry, Austin," I reply, "but Friday is Presentation Day. You'll need to present whatever you have prepared. Do the best you can. It's all about trying…"

The days wind down and presentations are the next day. The smell of glue sticks melting is in the air. Words are crafted and rehearsed. Glitter flies. I circulate and ensure that each learner is engaged and preparing. There is a sense of ownership and responsibility. There is also very little square footage left in the classroom. Projects are everywhere! Some students have last-minute requests:

> "Mrs. O, can you please bring some treats for my presentation? I know that the audience will be more interested if I give them a little quiz with prizes at the end."

> "Can I present just after lunch? My family tree cake would be perfect then."

Presentation Day

Presentation day always begins with much anticipation. The deadline promotes and amplifies expectations of self, of others. Nervous energy energizes the O-zone and is heard in laughter as well as arguing. Students take charge and begin a sign-up list on the whiteboard. The confident and strong can't wait to show off. Some don't bother signing up, hoping no one will notice and they won't have to present. (The rule is that if you need more time, you must negotiate with me and discuss a compromise prior to Presentation Day.) Still others are asking for a phone pass because needed props have been left behind at home. I stand back and smile. It's deeply satisfying to see learners in charge of their learning. They find meaning in experience — learning through reflection and doing. "With this project," says Andy, "I can see my work in motion and feel proud of it. It is always good to feel proud of your work. Finding facts on my own is better for my learning because if a teacher just tells me, then I will forget it in a week. I know where I came from now."

Each presentation reveals its presenter: strengths, gifts, vulnerabilities, and areas of weakness.

- Maddie loves to have great *Pow!* in her presentations. She has a connection to a local bakery and has negotiated to have them create a huge tree cake. Each leaf has the name of an ancestor in small, typed, carefully cut-out cards.
- Charis loves to build and is an extremely precise young man. He has carefully cut out and constructed a three-dimensional tree with cardboard parts. It resembles a jigsaw puzzle. Hanging like a decoration

"Tell me and I'll forget; show me and I may remember; involve me and I'll understand."

— Confucius

from each branch is an individual from his family. At the base are actual bits of tree root that lead to signs of the countries of his origin.

- Zack has drawn a huge tree on a double sheet of paper. With the support of his mom, he has pinned the names of his ancestors on the branches. He stands on the table to present and we are amazed at the size of his project!

Other students enjoy the telling part, making connections and telling the stories they have uncovered. Brianna brings precious family photographs we view as she tells.

Presentations took most of two days with a few short breaks. Quite a few parents joined us!

Each presentation stimulates the audience in different ways, ways often I would not ever have anticipated. This excites me and provokes me to consider, once again, that children have a much larger capacity to learn from one another than we think. (So, why do I still believe that growth and learning in the classroom depend so heavily on what *I* do and say?)

Assessment

I document the students' work with notes and photographs. This information gathering helps me to create an ongoing assessment of the concepts and ideas presented in the projects. The final summative assessment is given after the celebration. I also ask for peer feedback, both verbal and written, of each project. Pairs debate where on the rubric each presentation sits. Knowing they will be assessing each other encourages deep listening during the presentation and clarifying questions afterward. Those who didn't pay close attention are challenged by their partners during this process. I absolutely treasure these moments of conversation, negotiation, and sometimes irritation. The experience of peer assessment also helps the learners understand how they must use the rubric to support their opinions with evidence.

Celebration

A cultural potluck celebrates and completes our "Where did I come from?" challenge. Scones, pasta, and smoked salmon tickle our tastebuds.

"Hey, Mrs. O," calls Wesley over the lively party chatting. "I want to learn more about China now. Can we do our next project on a culture we are interested in?"

"I don't know, Wes. I had some other ideas. What do you think Levi?"

"Yeah, I am really interested in the world now. I want to keep learning more."

"Me too," chimes in Isaiah. "I want to learn how to hoop dance. I think my Dad will drum for me in my next presentation."

"Wow," I say. "That's just about all I can say. WOW!"

"Our class is not judgmental and it's positive. We care for each other and if we have problems we work them out. We also have talking circles if someone wants to share how they feel."

— Isaiah, age 12

A Parent's Reflection

I have read that kids who feel they belong and are attached to just one significant adult are much less likely to join gangs, do drugs, or otherwise go off the rails as they make their way toward adulthood.

Working in a community gives my son, who has a communication challenge, a sense of belonging to the group. With that belonging comes a sense of responsibility to the group: responsibility to participate, to contribute, to make relevant comments, to be ready to present a project — just like anybody else. Rather than being set aside for his differences and told that he can't, that he isn't capable, the expectation is for him to perform as a member of the community. And he does. He steps up to the plate again and again and challenges himself. And, as he does, he recognizes his own growth and his own abilities. Inside the sanctity of the O-zone, he is safe to be himself. A safe school is a place where all kids can be part of the group and are given the ability to recognize their own talents.

Through project-based learning my son has gained self-management skills that will serve him throughout his life — skills I wasn't sure I would ever see him develop. Here is a kid who balks at the idea of homework, who went head-to-head with a teacher over math sheets, but who now voluntarily stays in at recess or lunch or after school to get his work done to be ready to present. Not doing homework. Nope. Just being responsible to himself and to the group. ... I give project-based community learning an "E" — for "Essential."

— Diane Hutchinson, parent

8

Making Adaptations and Modifications to Improve Learning

Co-authored with
RANDY CRANSTON
and
LAURIE MESTON

"We need to focus on teaching kids, not just on special education. I am always advocating for instruction and instructional change. What I see is that we get caught up in pathologizing with labels and diagnosis and differences, rather than looking at how we are going to support learning."

— Randy Cranston, consultant

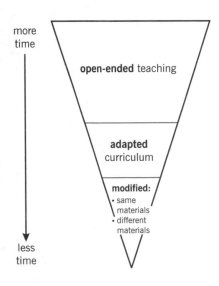

more time

open-ended teaching

adapted curriculum

modified:
• same materials
• different materials

less time

As noted in chapter 4, when teachers assume that all students will be included, they plan sequences and strategies that can be easily adapted or modified to meet the needs of all learners.

Adaptations are strategies that support students in achieving the learning outcomes of the curriculum. They may include adjustments to goals/ expectations, presentation, materials, assistance, environment, or evaluation. Adaptations are used to accommodate a student's needs so the student can achieve the learning outcomes of the subject or course and demonstrate mastery of concepts. Essentially, adaptations are a "best practice" in teaching. A student working on the learning outcomes of any grade or course level can be supported through use of adaptations. Some people think adaptations represent unfair advantages to students. In fact, the opposite is true, for if appropriate adaptations are not made, students might be unfairly penalized for having learning differences.

Modifications are changes to learning outcomes and assessment practices that result in students' learning goals and outcomes being substantially different from those of the curriculum. Modifications are specifically selected to address a student's special needs. The materials used can be the same or different from those of other students working with similar curriculum content. The goal in inclusive classrooms is to have all students working with similar curriculum content and similar materials.

The use of curriculum adaptation, wherever possible before modification, enhances the student's acceptance and inclusion in the classroom. It also keeps all doors open to the student and does not put a ceiling on the student's learning. Adaptations can be made with more ease than modifications, so using them reduces the teacher time needed to plan, organize, and implement multiple curricula.

When planning to meet the needs of any particular student within the classroom, you might find the following sequence of questions helpful.

1. Which learning outcomes can the student meet without any changes?
2. What adaptations can be made, and where can adaptations be made for the student to meet these learning outcomes?
3. Which, if any, learning outcomes will need to be modified? (Can this be done using the same classroom materials?)
4. Are there any times when the student will be working on different learning outcomes with different, but age-appropriate, materials?

The order of these questions is critical. Many times we think the student needs a separate curriculum or program when he or she really doesn't. Some students need modifications in one area but not others, or some modified and some adapted areas. If we overuse modifications the child will have a separate curriculum, and both the workload of the teacher and the exclusion of the student is increased.

It is always exciting to walk into a classroom and have to search to find the child who is working on an adapted program because that student is using the same materials as the rest of the students. If there is an adult helper in the room, she or he might be assisting many students with their work. There are lots of chances in this type of environment to capitalize on the social interaction of learning. The student can be taught to follow the model of the other children. That student learns from other students; can observe and try to copy other students' behavior. Observing, which is often a strong learning strategy for a student with special needs, allows the student to be successful.

The opposite — and distressing — scenario is walking into a classroom and quickly noticing one child working on different materials from all the other children, often separated from the other students, and perhaps sitting with an adult helper. In this environment the student becomes isolated from the classroom's social milieu.

Isolation often becomes the norm for students who are designated English as a Second Language (ESL). Considering that a frequent goal for such students is oral language fluency, it is hard to rationalize how this can happen when the English language models are removed from ESL students, who are left with packages of phonic worksheets.

Catherine Mills, an ESL/Resource teacher comments: "Over my years of working both as a classroom teacher and ESL/Resource teacher I have always been amazed at the ability of children to learn a new language. In a classroom that provides children with a wide variety of language-rich experiences, there is often little need to remove children because they are English as Second Language learners. If you watch carefully, you will see children helping each other learn new language through their play and rich reading, writing, and hands-on mathematical experiences. Children of all language backgrounds (and we have so many languages at our school) play, laugh, and learn together. Second-language learners grow through the security and love they feel in a caring classroom. Dividing children into skill 'levels', particularly as their language abilities start to blossom, seems unnatural to me."

"I know that the targeted students make more progress with support within the regular classroom."

— Catherine Feniak, principal/learning assistance teacher

Ways of Adapting Curriculum

Curriculum adaptations are needed for only certain students; there are many different ways to approach any needed adaptations. For ease of thinking about the ways to adapt, adaptations can be placed in the following categories: (1) goals/expectations, (2) environment, (3) presentation, (4) materials, (5) assistance, and (6) evaluation.

The following section describes some ideas for making adaptations in these six categories. Other ideas can be found at the end of the chapter. Many of these ideas were brainstormed by teachers at in-service sessions or during Individual Education Plan (IEP) meetings. These ideas — and others that teachers come up with when working with students and solution-finding with colleagues — help all of us to be more creative in assisting students in our classrooms.

1. Adapting Goals/Expectations

One of the initial adaptations to think about, and one of the easiest to accomplish, is to adapt the goals or expectations for a student. This does not require a lot of preplanning once a repertoire of ideas has been developed. For example, a child who has difficulty with written output can work on the same learning outcomes, but complete fewer questions or only those questions targeted to that student's goals.

There are many other ways of adapting goals and expectations. Some of these are

- reducing the number of goals in a unit for a particular student
- selecting concepts that relate to a specific student
- emphasizing functional tasks
- simplifying or extending the work
- removing time constraints or extending the time
- having the student read the introduction, main titles and subtitles, and summary instead of the whole chapter in a text
- using high-interest books
- allowing alternatives to the written form for the presentation of knowledge; for example, video, claymation, music, rap, drawing, diorama

See chapters 5 to 7 for examples of how students can begin to adapt for themselves when given the opportunity.

2. Adapting Environment

For most students, environments with lots of visual supports, including student work and teacher-prepared charts, allow them to be more successful. Use of these visual supports needs to be taught so students are able to make use of them. For some students, there is a need for more-directed or student-specific adaptations to help increase their success. Other students might need different environments within the day to enable them to focus during the time they are in the classroom. Inclusive practices do not mean that students must spend all day in the classroom.

If we are attending to student needs, we develop the program to meet these needs. We personalize their learning.

A student who has difficulty concentrating might benefit from sitting close to the teacher's desk, or working in a student carrel in the classroom during different parts of the day. Some teachers have carrels in the classroom as an option for any student who wants a quieter place to work. Students who have difficulties seeing the board, the screen used for overhead or LCD projection, or the interactive whiteboard benefit from sitting near the front of the classroom. Students who need to see the teacher speak or who need to read lips should be seated close to where the directions are given and away from glaring lights.

Some students require more specific adaptations, e.g., a wheelchair-accessible desk or a lip around the edge of the desk. Other students might require a larger table instead of a desk. One student we worked with focused better if he could stand rather than sit at a table; another benefited from having a wooden box under his feet so they were supported. Another idea, brainstormed by a frustrated teacher for a student with organizational difficulties, was to tie the student's pencil to her desk so that she couldn't lose it. Collegial or school-based team meetings allow us to come up with a wide range of thinking to consider what might work, and they don't block our thoughts with "yes, but..."

A student who can't readily concentrate for long periods of time sometimes benefits from working in many environments. Some students might have timetables that require them to be in different places to do different jobs relating to their IEP or program plan. For example, after a block of time in the classroom, a student might be expected to go to an early primary classroom to listen to and read to a younger child; then the student's next job might be to work in the library. A student who needs to transition from home to the school environment or who needs purposeful movement might be expected first thing in the morning to collect all the attendance forms from each classroom and return them to the school office. For one student, collecting attendance meant working on the goals of matching (the staff picture on wall beside classroom door to the picture on her monitoring clipboard), letter recognition (matching the first letter of teacher's name to the first letter on her monitoring clipboard), number recognition (copying the classroom number in the space provided on her monitoring clipboard), and so on. Adapted and personalized timetables such as this can be very useful for students with behavioral difficulties.

3. Adapting Presentation

A typical strategy in many classrooms is for the teacher to make a general presentation to all students, and to follow up with individual students or groups. Some students need an adapted presentation; however, many classroom teachers make adaptations to their presentations as part of their typical day-to-day teaching. When a teacher thinks about adapting presentation two questions could be considered:

• What are the key points to remember when presenting effectively to the entire class?

• If there are adaptations in presentation I need to make for individual students, what are they?

Some ideas to think about when planning for presentation to the entire class:
• demonstrating and modeling the task (I do it, we do it, you do it)
• using graphic organizers to assist students in understanding how different concepts connect
• building criteria with students so that they understand what they are working toward
• using rhyme, rhythm, songs, patterns, video clips, and drama as alternative ways to present materials
• presenting with an overhead, an LCD projector, PowerPoint, or an interactive whiteboard so that students hear and see the materials being discussed
• putting directions, examples, and homework in the same place on the board each day so that students know where to look for clarification

When thinking about adaptations in presentation for individual students, it is important to look at the strategies that make the greatest difference to student engagement. Some students require the directions to be broken down into a number of steps, others need hand signals, sign language, or instructions to be repeated. Other students might respond best to having parts of the directions in their texts highlighted or underlined or to the use of concrete materials. For some students, just standing close to them when giving the directions or putting your hand on their shoulder might be all that is needed to help them concentrate on the directions given. In any case, the key question is this: "What adaptations can I make in what I am presenting to increase student engagement with the material?"

4. Adapting Materials

The majority of students can learn well using common classroom materials, but not all students need to use the same materials all the time to achieve the same learning outcomes. For some students, a better learner/material match can significantly change their ability to learn.

In many schools, students who have difficulty with writing due to difficulties with written output or fine motor skills are using computers in the classroom. Doing this has helped students with note-taking, organization, writing, and the ability to read back what is written. There are a number of assistive technology supports available to help students with communication, reading, and writing, including Kurzweil 3000™, WordCue, Communicate:, Inspiration® software, Clicker 5, PictureSET, Boardmaker®, electronic text, talking story books and trade books, and Internet-based text materials. Some students with visual impairments or fine motor challenges benefit from having materials enlarged. Other students find it helpful if their notebooks or paper are adapted slightly; for example, if a student has difficulty with printing or writing, raised-line paper or colored lines can be helpful. Graph paper works well for a student who has difficulty with lining up numbers.

"[Students in the classroom] start to extrapolate the idea that everyone learns in different ways and at different rates, that we can all still be kind to one another, and that we are all better at some things than others. We are all better prepared for life beyond school and accepting that differences are natural."

— Cynthia Higgins, special education assistant

Sometimes students benefit from adapted devices, such as left-handed or hand-over-hand scissors, chalk holders, pencil grippers, date or number stamps, corner pouches to hold pages down, or a recipe stand to hold books or single pages upright. Color-coded notebooks or highlighters can help students who have difficulty organizing materials. Other students with reading or math challenges might be supported by having a number line or alphabet taped to their desk to assist them when they write. For students who have difficulty with written output, photocopying another student's notes or using carbonless copy paper can free that student to focus on the discussion or presentation. Many of these adaptations are easy to set up, yet can make a big difference to a student's success in the classroom.

5. Adapting Assistance

Assistance can come from many people who are part of a classroom — the teacher, peers, an older student, the support teacher, the teaching assistant, and volunteers. Our premise is that the support teacher is working in collaboration with the classroom teacher and knows all the students in the classroom. The responsibility for programming for students rests with the classroom teacher in conjunction with the support teacher. These teachers consult each other, plan together, solution-find, and jointly strive to teach all children in the classroom. If a paraprofessional is available to assist, the paraprofessional needs to work to support the classroom program and students within that program rather than being attached to one particular student.

In looking at the level of assistance needed for a student, move from the least adaptation to the most; for example, begin working with a peer in the classroom or an older peer tutor before considering assistance from a paraprofessional. When assistance is looked at this way, it forces us to be creative and to think about independence versus dependence for the student.

A peer assistant in the classroom can assist in many ways: as a model, helper, organization assistant, reader, scribe, question answerer, and tutor. Older tutors can often be trained and can possibly receive course credit for assisting students in academic areas. They might read to students, listen to students read and ask them questions, run through flashcards, support fluency practice, or scribe a story. For example, one student with technological expertise can teach another student how to use a program to support written output. Both students benefit significantly from this tutoring situation. The student with the technological expertise reinforces his or her knowledge, figures out how to share his or her expertise, and feels good about sharing it with another student. The student with the written-output difficulty becomes able to share ideas with others with greater ease.

It is also important to consider the student with specific learning or behavioral needs as a peer assistant. Many times, a student with special needs benefits more from helping than from being helped, and can work with younger students in math, reading, or centre time. Such students might also be library monitors, score keepers, or attendance collectors.

When making decisions about areas of assistance, be sure to consider student strengths; for example, when a student with significant reading challenges took on the responsibility of setting up sound-system materials for all school assemblies because of an interest in, love of, and expertise in technology, it was amazing to see how the student read various manuals when he had to troubleshoot.

6. Adapting Evaluation

There are many ways of finding out what a student knows beyond the typical standard test format. There are both exemplary group evaluation practices and individually appropriate practices based on student need.

Some group practices include developing criteria with the whole class and then using these criteria when evaluating completed work. Once students understand and have worked with the criteria, they can use them in self-evaluation. Many teachers also use portfolio assessments and have students reflect on their work, set goals each term, chart progress, and evaluate themselves.

Adaptations in evaluation need to take into account students' learning needs. Some students might require a scribe for answering questions. The scribe does not need to be an adult; it can be another student. This support is critical when a teacher is evaluating content knowledge. A student with writing challenges might understand the content concepts and be unable to communicate them in writing. With a scribe, such students can show what they know, and the teacher can better evaluate the students' knowledge in this area. Other adaptations in evaluation can include reading test questions aloud to a student who has difficulties in reading, and having a student who has difficulties in writing draw answers or record them on tape or digitally. See chapters 5 and 6 for more examples of adapting evaluation.

For some students all that is required is more time to complete the test or the opportunity to write the test in an different location, such as another room or at home. For some students, knowing that they can rewrite the test if they don't do well the first time is all that is required. One teacher devised an easy way to assess a student on specific goals using the same test as the other students by highlighting the specific questions the student needed to answer.

Classroom-Based Curriculum Adaptations and Modifications

Specific classroom examples help build our understanding of ways to support learning in our own classrooms. These examples demonstrate how we try to adapt as much as possible, even for those students with significant challenges. We also try to work toward independence at all times, and are pleased to see that students, once having learned how to do a task, often can work independently without having an adult by their side — a very important achievement!

Math, Grade 6

The area of study is fractions. Many of the students are independently working on practice questions on multiplication of fractions, some with manipulatives and some in groups. One student's sheet is enlarged because she has challenges with written output. Two students are doing only the odd-numbered questions, as it takes them longer to complete the computations. One student is working with a designated partner, as this helps him focus. These are all examples of *adaptations* of materials, goals, presentation, and assistance.

One child is working on a *modified* curriculum. He is using the same sheet as his peers, but is focusing on two of his IEP goals: matching and recognizing numbers from 1 to 10, and recognizing shapes. Today he is to circle the number 6, to draw a square around the number 7, and to draw a triangle around the number 8 wherever they appear. This is cued for him at the top of the page. He is also to match all the appearances of each of these numbers with each other by drawing a line to join them. He is doing this task independently without the assistance of a teaching assistant.

Spelling, Grade 3/4 Combined

Students are practicing individual spelling words that have been teacher- or student-selected. There are a different number of words for different students. Students have been taught various spelling strategies to use when practicing their words, including closure activities; look, say, cover, write, check; sketching; tracing; verbal rehearsal; rhyming; dictating words to partners; and writing words in sentences. This method of implementing a spelling program could be described as an *adaptation* of a traditional spelling program in terms of materials and presentation; however, as it is the program being implemented by the teacher, the only adaptation is in goals (some students are working on fewer words or more words than might be determined as the norm for Grades 3 or 4). One specific student with written-output difficulties is working with adapted material in that he is practicing his words on raised-line paper.

One student is working on a *modified* spelling program. She is listening to a peer read and practice his spelling words, and is writing the first letter of each word as part of her IEP goal of representing letters of the alphabet.

Language Arts, Grade 8: Readers Workshop

All the students are reading books of their own choosing, from a selection of ten different choices. These books represent a range of difficulty. The students meet in small groups to share their responses. The purpose of the activity is to connect personal experience with the material being read and thereby enhance comprehension of text. Three students are listening to their book on tape. Two of these students often draw rather than write their responses, and typically summarize orally what they have read. There is a visual prompt by the listening station: "What does this remind you of?" All students are included in the small-group discussions. These are examples of *adaptations* in assistance, materials, and evaluation.

Language Arts, Grade 5: Class Read-Aloud Novel

The teacher is reading a novel about slavery to the class. Students have a four-square response sheet with the following squares: *(1) surprises, (2) laws about slavery, (3) description of where slaves were almost caught, (4) types of food slaves ate.* As the teacher reads, students make notes in the appropriate sections. Two students are drawing their responses. One student who is visually impaired has had her sheet enlarged to 11" X 17"; another student who is physically challenged and cannot hold a pen is dictating his responses into a hand-held recorder. These are examples of the *adaptation* of materials and evaluation.

Two students are working on a *modified* curriculum. One has difficulty listening for four different areas. His goals have been modified and he is listening for only *(3) description of where slaves were almost caught.* Another student who is physically and mentally challenged is sitting at a tilt-top desk, using a stamp and making a mark in square *(4) types of food slaves ate* every time he hears a food mentioned.

Planning for All Students in the Class

When planning a unit or series of lessons, the classroom teacher decides on the critical learning outcomes and the ways that the students will demonstrate their understanding of these learning outcomes. The classroom teacher, often working with the support teacher, then decides which of the learning outcomes can be met by all students and which students will need some adaptations and/or modifications to be successful in their learning.

With the specific students in mind, the classroom teacher, in consultation with the support teacher, can make adjustments to the learning outcomes (goals/expectations), environment, presentation, or materials, and to the way the students will demonstrate their understanding (evaluation).

The example that follows outlines learning outcomes for a Grade 6 class in social studies. Brian and Serena are students in this class who require classroom-based Individual Education Plans to support their learning. The Program Analysis Worksheet is used to plan for both students and the Critical Activities Matrix is used to plan for Serena. The Program Analysis Worksheet outlines adaptations or modifications for each of the students. It is a particularly effective planning tool to use with students like Brian, whose learning needs are not that discrepant from his peers. The Critical Activities Matrix is used in planning for Serena, a student whose learning outcomes differ significantly from those of her peers.

Learning Outcomes: Grade 6 Social Studies

Prescribed Learning Outcomes	Suggested Achivement Indicators
Skills and Processes of Social Studies • interpret graphs, tables, aerial photos, and various types of maps	• locate and map continents, oceans, and seas using photos and various types of maps, simple grids, scales, and legends • locate the prime meridian, equator, Tropic of Cancer, Tropic of Capricorn, Arctic Circle, and Antarctic Circle on a globe or map of the world • recognize the relationship between time zones and lines of longitude • compare how graphs, table, aerial photos, and maps represent information • represent the same information in two or more graphic forms (e.g., graphs, tables, thematic maps)
Human and Physical Environment • assess the relationship between cultures and their environments	• on a map locate major geographic features (e.g., mountains, lakes, rivers, oceans) of selected countries • use maps, climagraphs, and other resources to identify the major environmental features (e.g., forests, deserts, plains, precipitation, temperature) of selected countries and regions studied • give examples of how geographical features have affected development of cultures in selected countries and regions (e.g., major economic activities, transportation methods, shelter, agriculture, artistic expression, recreational activities)

Adaptations for Brian Using a Program Analysis Worksheet

Brian is able to understand directions and participate expressively in discussions. He can learn new concepts and is able to focus his attention on tasks. He can read a few high-frequency words as well as some personal words. He can print his first name and expresses his thinking in writing using phonetic approximations and drawings. He likes being in school and works hard.

Although Brian can meet some of the learning outcomes related to the Skills and Processes and the Human and Physical Environment sections of Grade 6 social studies, he requires some adaptations in order to be successful. As seen on the Program Analysis Worksheet (see page 91), Brian needs to have a peer read him the directions. He also needs enlarged paper-and-pencil activities on which to print his name, to cut and paste the names of water bodies, and to match symbols of environmental features. In addition to the adaptations, Brian is working on individual learning outcomes. Some of these include legibly printing his first name, reading and recognizing Canada within the continent of North America, and increasing his reading vocabulary.

How to Use a Program Analysis Worksheet

See page 141 for a reproducible Program Analysis Worksheet.

The Program Analysis Worksheet is a working, classroom-based Individual Education Plan. It is used to adapt and modify the learning outcomes for a unit or theme. Typically, it is most effective when used for a student who can meet some of the classroom learning outcomes, but requires adaptations/modifications to be successful on all the learning outcomes.

Follow these steps for using the Program Analysis Worksheet. The purpose is to develop and implement a plan that focuses on including the student in the classroom program.

1. List the class learning outcomes in the left-hand column. Learning outcomes can be cut and pasted from overviews, curriculum guides, or instructional resource packages (IRPs). Highlight any learning outcomes that the student can meet without any adaptations or modifications.

2. List evaluation methods/culminating activities for class learning outcomes in the Evaluation column. Highlight any evaluation processes that are appropriate for the student.

3. List any individual learning outcomes for the student in column 6. These might include outcomes related to the curricular area; e.g., *recognize and read the names of all continents*. Or they might include comments that are more focused on behavioral/social needs; e.g., *raise hand to participate in class discussions* or *take turns during math games*.

4. To adapt or modify the class learning outcomes, examine each class learning outcome in column 1 and ask the following question: *Can the student achieve the learning outcome if I adapt/modify the goal, environment, presentation, materials, assistance, and/or evaluation?* While doing this, keep in mind the individual learning outcomes for the student.

5. For each learning outcome, write general adaptations or modifications that might work for the student in column 4: e.g., *complete the even numbered questions; reduce the number of items required; group with reading partner; provide enlarged photocopied pages; provide example at top of page; scribe answers on test.*

6. Use these general adaptations/modifications as a guide to adapt specific strategies and activities to support the student's learning. These specific adaptations can be noted in the teacher's daybook beside the strategy or activity.

7. Determine who will be responsible for the adaptations or modifications: the classroom teacher (CT), peers (P), the support teacher (ST), the teaching assistant (TA), parents (PA), or volunteers (V). Note this in the appropriate column.

8. Complete the Evaluation column. Put a check mark in the As Is column if the student can complete the activity along with the other students.

PROGRAM ANALYSIS WORKSHEET

© Cranston/Meston, Maple Ridge

Name: Brian

Curricular Area: Social Studies

Date Initiated: January 2011

Review Date: March 2011

Class Learning Outcomes *highlight appropriate objectives	Evaluation	As Is	Is It Appropriate? with adapted goals environment, presentation, materials, assistance, evaluation	Person Responsible	Individual Learning Outcomes (materials, criteria, review date)	Evaluation Comments (date achieved)
Assess the relationship between cultures and their environments • on a map locate major geographic features (mountains, rivers, lakes, oceans) of selected country	ongoing activities		• reading partner reads legends, keys, labels Evaluation: see below	CT Peer	• put first name on all papers	
• using maps, climagraphs, and other resources, identify the major environmental features (e.g. forests, deserts, plains, precipitation, temperature) of selected countries and regions studied	culminating activity		• provide him with symbols to match environmental features • enlarge materials as needed	CT	• read and recognize one river and lake • identify symbols by name	
Interpret graphs, tables, aerial photos, and various types of maps • locate and map continents, oceans, and seas using simple grids, scales, and legends	ongoing activities		• with partner • reduce number of features to locate • label vs. map	Peer CT	• read and recognize Canada within North America	
• locate the prime meridian, equator, Tropic of Cancer, Tropic of Capricorn, Arctic Circle, and Antarctic Circle on a globe or map of the world	culminating activity		Evaluation			
• recognize the relationship between time zones and lines of longitude;	ongoing activities		• have peer/adult read key of geographic features to Brian	CT/Peer		
• compare how graphs, tables, aerial photos and maps represent information • represent the same information in two or more graphic forms (e.g., graphs, tables, thematic maps	culminating activity		• provide names of six bodies of water to cut and paste • Arctic Circle and Antarctic Circle only	CT/TA		

Adaptations for Serena Using a Program Analysis Worksheet and a Critical Activities Matrix

Serena is able to verbalize about twelve words. She can recognize the numbers 1 to 4. She is working on making appropriate sounds at appropriate times, sitting with a partner, and staying with the group for whole-class activities. A paraprofessional is in the classroom for about 80% of the day to provide assistance.

Serena cannot meet the class learning outcomes independently or with minor adaptations. Serena's plan needs to be based on her individual learning outcomes. Some of the goals that she is trying to meet are

- Verbalizing a greater number of words
- Increasing her use of appropriate sounds
- Increasing the length of time on task
- Identifying and matching colors
- Identifying and matching shapes
- Following simple one-step directions
- Recognizing number sequences of 1, 2, 3, 4, 5
- Grasping small objects with pincer grasp
- Developing fine motor skills
- Unscrewing and tightening jar lids

All these learning outcomes can be worked on in social studies using classroom-based materials and resources. Serena can work in small groups or with a partner with the same materials, but with different goals and expectations.

Two formats for planning for Serena's learning (IEP) are illustrated: the Program Analysis Worksheet on page 93 and the Critical Activities Matrix on page 94. The Matrix is most useful for students whose learning outcomes differ significantly from those of their peers. In planning, teachers typically use one form or the other.

How to Use a Critical Activities Matrix

See page 142 for a reproducible Critical Activities Matrix.

The Critical Activities Matrix can be used instead of the Program Analysis Worksheet. It is most useful for students whose goals and learning outcomes are significantly different from other students in the classroom. The form allows the teacher to integrate the student's individual learning outcomes into the classroom structure. In this way, the teacher can easily see where and how the child can participate in the daily classroom activities and routines. Such participation promotes inclusion and acceptance, looking at natural ways that peers can be of assistance. Using a Critical Activities Matrix encourages all involved not to automatically use parallel programs, but instead to think about how the classroom activity and the student's learning outcomes can be connected.

Follow these steps to use the Critical Activities Matrix. The purpose is to develop and implement a plan that focuses on including the student in the classroom program.

1. Enlarge a blank Critical Activities Matrix to an 11" × 17" piece of paper, as this provides more space to write ideas in the matrix squares.

PROGRAM ANALYSIS WORKSHEET

© Cranston/Meston, Maple Ridge

Name: Serena

Curricular Area: Social Studies

Date Initiated: January 2011

Review Date: March 2011

Class Learning Outcomes *highlight appropriate objectives	Evaluation	As Is	Is It Appropriate? with adapted goals environment, presentation, materials, assistance, evaluation	Person Responsible	Individual Learning Outcomes (materials, criteria, review date)	Evaluation Comments (date achieved)
Assess the relationship between cultures and their environments • on a map locate major geographic features (mountains, rivers, lakes, oceans) of selected country	ongoing activities		GENERIC ADAPTATIONS can be used for a number of her individual learning outcomes		• increase number of words she can verbalize	
• using maps, climagraphs, and other resources, identify the major environmental features (e.g. forests, deserts, plains, precipitation, temperature) of selected countries and regions studied	culminating activity		• pair with partner (buddy) wherever possible, particularly in activities where she can imitate sounds • have her imitate initial sounds in words: names of geographic features, continents, oceans, etc. • Serena will hand out materials to group members, keep pencils in jar to unscrew	peer TA peer	• identify and match colors • follow simple directions • increase length of time on task (stay with group)	
Interpret graphs, tables, aerial photos, and various types of maps • locate and map continents, oceans, and seas using simple grids, scales, and legends	ongoing activities		• have buddy ask her to point to colored geographic features: continents, oceans, legends, etc. • during mapping activities, have her focus on concrete activities; e.g. map of classroom. She can cut and paste classroom features; e.g., desks, bulletin boards.	peer CT/TA	• develop fine motor skills: cutting with scissors, pasting on paper, grasping small objects (pincer grasp), unscrewing/tightening jar lids	
• locate the prime meridian, equator, Tropic of Cancer, Tropic of Capricorn, Arctic Circle, and Antarctic Circle on a globe or map of the world	culminating activity		• have her number tasks on group responses	peer	• recognize in sequence 1, 2, 3, 4	
• recognize the relationship between time zones and lines of longitude;	ongoing activities		• have her recognize numbers from time zones, graphs, etc. Evaluation: focus on individual, not class, outcomes	TA CT		
• compare how graphs, tables, aerial photos and maps represent information • represent the same information in two or more graphic forms (e.g., graphs, tables, thematic maps	culminating activity		Create a Map: have her match and label colors and objects by pasting pictures of objects on classroom map and/or matching colors on map of the world Follow Directions: have Serena move marker from colored continent to colored continent on map	CT CT		

93

Critical Activities Matrix

© Ives/Meston, Maple Ridge

Name: Serena

Date: January 2011　　　　**Review Date:** March 2011

Individual Learning Outcomes	Classroom Activities						
	Arrival	Class Meeting	Language Arts	Recess/Lunch	Math	Music PE, Art	Science/Social Studies
Increasing her use of appropriate sounds at appropriate times and the number of words she can verbalize	"Hi___" "Hello" How are you?" "Good morning" Adults and Serena talking	Ask yes/no questions	• responds to "work time" "picture"	• responds to "outside" "eat"	• responds to "one to five" word approximation	• responds to "cut" "paste"; color words • hums in music, cheers in PE	• responds to "scissors" "glue" "help"; initial sounds for continents, oceans, etc.
Increase length of time on task		• sits on chair beside friend	Use timer and work/break structure	• stays with activity once chosen (outside)	Use timer and work/break structure, provide tasks on numbered cards		Use timer and work/break structure
Identify and match colors	Color code/label coat hook • matches color on agenda		Use color-coded notebooks	• colors on adventure playground	Color-coded book	• labels colors	• matches colors of geographic features – continents, oceans, etc
Identify and match shapes	• matches shapes with those on personal agenda	Put shape on Serena's chair for her to match				Use shapes, symbols for PE stations	
Follow simple one-step directions	• sees/recognizes number sequences	• gives books to specific person	• hands out color-coded notebooks to colored tables (matching)	e.g., "Get red ball"	• hands out materials: "Give book to ___"	"cut" "paste" "line up" "stop" "come here"	"cut" "paste" "put here"
Recognize number sequences of 1, 2, 3, 4, 5	Take shape cards numbered 1 to 5 and put beside class agenda		• counts number of books handed out at each table		• does matching/ connecting in sequence activities, games • finds amounts	Number stations in PE	• puts numbers beside matching and cutting tasks; therefore does in sequence
Develop fine motor skills: cutting, pasting, grasping small objects (pincer grasp), unscrewing/ tightening jar lids	Have numbers in jar to unscrew and tighten	• pulls meeting topic from jar she has to unscrew	Keep game chips in jar for her to open/ close • distributes table materials		• cuts out numbers, places in appropriate place	Put PE game choices in jar	• cuts out classroom objects and pastes on map
Increase independence: unscrew and tighten jar lids	See above	See above	See above				

Note: • indicates student behaviors; notes without bullets indicate adult tasks.

2. List individual student learning outcomes in the left-hand column. Typically, these outcomes are not subjects, units, or specific themes, but are instead the goals that teachers/parents/students have established at the IEP meeting.

3. List daily activities, including recess and lunch, as well as unit/theme strategies and activities across the top of the matrix. You can follow the plan of the day, or group some subjects together as illustrated in the example on page 94.

4. Connect each learning outcome with each activity and write the ideas in the matrix squares. Think creatively. This often works best if you brainstorm with a partner. Ask yourselves questions: for example, "How can a child learn to identify and match shapes during most periods of the day?" Then begin to brainstorm ideas. Don't stop to analyze them, just get the ideas out — some will work, others won't. Could the child's coat hook have a specific shape beside it? Could his or her cubby be designated by a shape? Could the child's notebooks be coded with a shape? Could he or she hand out papers to other students that are in file folders with different shapes on them? Could the student's work be kept in file folders coded by shape as well as words? Could each period of the day be denoted by a shape on the class agenda? Could storage bins in the PE equipment room be coded by shapes? Could rooms in the school be marked with a shape for the child to match attendance sheets to the room shape (and number)? Could numbers for matching tasks in math be written on shape cards? Could you use a stop-sign shape to designate stopping for different activities? Once a group starts brainstorming, the list can be endless.

Adaptations are vitally important if children are to succeed in school and belong in the regular classroom. Many of the adaptations that we make for children are simple, just part of what teachers do every day; others are more complex and take more time to develop. We have learned that developing any necessary adaptations is much easier and the outcomes are more creative when the planning is done with someone else.

A Summary of Ways to Make Adaptations to Improve Learning begins on the next page. They are grouped in the six categories discussed in this chapter. You can use these ideas to stimulate thinking and assist you in coming up with new ideas.

Summary of Ways to Make Adaptations to Improve Learning

*Adapted from School District No. 42 (Maple Ridge/Pitt Meadows), British Columbia

These ideas were brainstormed by teachers at a variety of workshops and during planning meetings.

Adapting Goals/Expectations

- Reduce number of goals in the unit for student to work on.
- Decide upon smaller amounts of work, odd or even questions.
- Reduce number of concepts to be learned.
- Select concepts that relate to student.
- Simplify/extend the work.
- Emphasize functional tasks.
- Use high-interest books.
- Remove time constraints/extend time.
- Read introduction, summary, and main titles vs. whole text.
- Have alternatives for the way knowledge can be represented.

Adapting Environment

Classroom Environment and Position in Room
- Consider student's senses: vision, hearing, smell, touch.
- Seat at front or back of room
- Seat away from noise (lights, street, hall, computer)
- Use carrel/screens.
- Seat with back to window
- Seat by teacher
- Manage lighting; e.g., light on desk, back to window, etc.

Cooperative Grouping
- Seating at desk
- Wheelchair accessible desk
- Laptop desk
- Lip on side of desk
- Desk with flip-up top
- Tilt-top desk
- Use larger table instead of desk.
- Have student stand at desk instead of sitting.
- Use light box to work at.
- Provide box for feet so they are supported.

Adapting Environment

General Organization
- A lazy susan to organize desk
- Drawers beside desk
- Soup can for pencils
- Bookends/bookholder to hold books on desk
- Tie pencil to desk.
- Attach pencil to student with extension key ring.
- Have list of items to complete on desk.
- Have timetable on desk, in notebooks (pictorial or written).
- Have student goal on desk.
- Reduce excess paper and materials on desk.
- Color-code class duotangs.
- Have student come in ten minutes early and go over day plan.
- Use headphones to quiet outbursts.
- Seat on mat at circle time
- Seat on chair at circle time
- Create legitimate opportunities to move.
- Designate places in the classroom for quiet time, special materials.

Different Environments
Have student assist in another classroom for short periods of time, e.g., help teach PE to a primary class, stack chairs for the Kindergarten classroom, read to a younger buddy, or do a job in the office or library.

Adapting Presentation

Strategies for the Whole Class
- Demonstrate and model (I do it, we do it, you do it).
- Use graphic organizers.
- Build criteria with students.
- Be explicit about expectations.
- Give oral instructions from different places in the classroom.
- Use rhyme, rhythm, songs, patterning, drama for presentation.
- Keep in mind length of teacher talk (primary 5–7 minutes; intermediate 7–12 minutes).

Pembroke Publishers © 2011 *Learning in Safe Schools, revised edition* by Faye Brownlie and Judith King ISBN 978-1-55138-266-1

Adapting Presentation — *continued*

- Modify pace — speak more slowly or more quickly.
- Encourage students to make eye contact with presenter.
- Break information into steps.
- Write down instructions.
- Always put specific information, such as homework, directions, examples, in the same place on the board.
- Use pictures.
- Use different color chalk/pens.
- Use overhead, LCD projector, interactive whiteboard.
- Use multi-sensory examples.
- Give structured overview; students fill in the blanks while listening.
- Use two-column notes.
- Involve students in presentation — concept mapping.

Strategies for Individual Needs

- Use hand signals/sign language.
- Separate visual/auditory information.
- Repeat instructions.
- Pre-teach vocabulary.
- Stand close to student.
- Ask student to repeat the instructions.
- Have peer repeat instructions.
- Use concrete materials.
- Videotape for later review.
- Complete first example with student.
- Simplify instructions.
- Provide additional time to preview materials, complete tasks, take tests.
- Audiorecord instructions.
- Use social stories.
- Highlight key points in textbooks — student just reads these points.
- If student has visual impairments, use high contrast materials and determine where and when they can see best.

Adapting Materials

- Dictate to a scribe.
- Audiorecord answers.
- Draw pictures.
- Cut pictures from magazines.
- Dioramas; build a model.

Adapting Materials — *continued*

- Laptop, computer
- Assistive technology: Clicker 5, Kurzweil 3000™, WordCue, PictureSET, Boardmaker®, Inspiration® software, Communicate:
- Electronic text, talking story books and trade books
- Internet-based textual material
- Graphic-based writing software
- Voice-recognition software
- Hand-held word processor (like a laptop)
- Switch access
- Hand-held translators
- Use overhead transparency sheets, paper clipped to the textbook pages, so student can write answers to questions in the book.
- Use manipulatives.
- Use calculator — talking type, larger size.
- Use colored pens to record thinking at different times.

Adapted Devices

- Scissors — have many types available.
- Chalk holders
- Pencil grippers
- Highlighters
- Bingo markers to indicate choice
- Date stamp, number stamps
- Dycem®, Velcro®
- Corner pouches to hold pages down
- No-carbon-required (NCR) paper (NCR)
- Number line, alphabet on desk
- Erasable pens
- Recipe stand to hold books upright, or single sheets
- Vegetable bins to hold materials at table

Adapting Page Set-up

- Line indicators
- Different types of paper
- Paper with mid lines
- Raised-line paper
- Paper with red and green lines
- Provide more white space to put answers.
- Highlight directions.
- Cover sections of text/sheet.
- Provide greater contrast: blue ink is hard to see.
- Extra large print
- Work on bigger paper.

Pembroke Publishers © 2011 *Learning in Safe Schools, revised edition* by Faye Brownlie and Judith King ISBN 978-1-55138-266-1

Adapting Materials — *continued*

- Use sticky notes to create text for pictures in reading materials.

Adapting Assistance

Support Teacher

- Consultation
- Supports teacher to teach every child well.
- Works primarily in classroom with teacher.
- Problem-solves with teacher.

Peer Assistant

- As model
- As helper
- As organization assistant
- As question answerer
- As reader
- As scribe
- As peer tutor

Peer Assistant (Student with Challenges)

- Helps younger student in reading, math, or general assistant. Look at student's strengths.
- Helps in school: in office, in library, cares for plants, as score keeper, hands out books, sharpens pencils.

Teacher Assistants (Paraprofessionals)

- Assigned to school, to classroom; works with whole class.
- Facilitates ownership by classroom teacher and follows teacher direction.

Consultants/Itinerant Teachers

- Work in classroom.
- Model for teacher.
- Use curriculum as guide.

Community Support

- High-school students
- Volunteer grandparents
- Parent volunteers

Adapting Materials — *continued*

Communication Tools

- Homework books/student planners
- Back-and-forth communication books

Adapting Evaluation

- Self-evaluation
- Peer evaluation
- KWL — know, want to know, learned
- Have students show knowledge in different ways.
- Develop criteria with students.
- Use different criteria to evaluate.
- Keep work samples.
- Portfolio assessment
- Do spot checks.
- Set small goals.
- Use video.

Tests

- Use a scribe.
- Oral test
- Have someone read test questions.
- Test on modified objectives (highlight questions student needs to answer).
- Let students use calculator; draw pictures; take test home; take test in another room.
- No-time test
- Open-book test
- Provide more space to write.
- Delete some of the options.
- Enlarge print.
- Audiorecord test directions/questions.
- Audiorecord answers.
- Provide opportunities to retake tests or parts of tests.

Reporting

- Give work habit grade/comment.
- Attach anecdotal comments.
- Use same format for other students.
- Use * to note modification.
- Focus on growth.

Pembroke Publishers © 2011 *Learning in Safe Schools, revised edition* by Faye Brownlie and Judith King ISBN 978-1-55138-266-1

Part Three

Taking "Ownership" of All Students

9

Creating a Resource Model

With thanks to Kim Boettcher, Catherine Feniak, Jeri Jackovac, Barb McLaughlin, Catherine Mills, Shelley Moore, and Leyton Schnellert

The movement toward full inclusion of students with special needs into regular classrooms precipitated an examination of teachers' roles. Classroom teachers began to say, "I can't meet with all these different support people about students in my classroom." The classroom teacher might have to meet with many different resource people: the learning assistance teacher; the English as a Second Language (ESL) teacher; the reading teacher; the counselor; members of the autism team; the First Nations Support Worker; teachers of students with learning disabilities, hearing impairments, visual impairments, behavior disorders, mental challenges, multiple handicaps; the occupational therapist, the physical therapist, the physiotherapist, and/or the nurse. Teachers were becoming overwhelmed by the support contacts.

Many resource personnel also began to question the effectiveness of their roles. A learning assistance teacher might have forty-five students on a caseload and twelve classroom teachers to consult with. Many learning assistance teachers would say: "I'm only bandaging," "I have no time to talk with teachers," "There is no carryover to the classroom." As budgets decreased, an additional concern was frequently raised: "I am stretched so thin that I have time to deal with only the students with the most significant learning needs. I never seem to get to see the students who need short-term assistance or general adaptations to their programming in order for them to be successful. These students are falling through the cracks."

Resource staff began to compare roles and wonder how they could assist each other. For example, in schools where the teachers of students with significant learning challenges might work with ten children, and the learning assistance teacher might work with forty-five children, discussions began as to whether or not they could combine their resources and share the load more effectively.

The Move toward a Non-Categorical Resource Team Model

Many teams now work generically. The time allotted to the school for ESL, learning assistance, high-incidence support (learning disabilities, behavior, mild mental challenges, gifted and talented), and low-incidence support (e.g., more significant mental and behavioral difficulties, multiple handicaps, autism) is combined and used to hire teachers and special education assistants who can work with all students — those with identified special needs *and* all the other students in the classroom. There is a philosophical shift when you make this move to a non-categorical model.

To the left is an example of how you might staff a resource team. The school begins by looking at the amount of staffing they are given and adding all of the time allotments together. For example, the school might have the equivalent of two full-time resource teachers. In some districts, it might have the flexibility to make choices, such as 1.5 teachers and a full-time teaching assistant. The decision of how to allocate staffing is decided based on strengths and needs and on the context of the school and district.

Resource Team Staffing

learning assistance	.7
ESL	.7
special education (low-incidence, behavior, etc.)	.5
gifted/talented	.1
Total Teaching Staff	2.0

Elementary

In an elementary school where there are two full-time resource teachers and fourteen classes, the resource teachers might choose to organize their service delivery in some of the following ways:

- Each teacher has seven divisions.
- One teacher is responsible for primary, the other for intermediate.
- The school-based team (after a class review) might look at the needs of each classroom and decide that one teacher will have six divisions, because there are more needs in those classes, while the other teacher has eight.
- They may look at their own expertise: the teacher with more expertise in ESL might take the classes with the greatest number of students who are new Canadians; the teacher with more expertise in supporting behavior concerns might take the classrooms where there are more students with behavioral challenges; the resource teacher who has strengths working with new teachers might take the classrooms with new teachers.

Secondary

In a secondary school with two full-time resource teachers, they might decide to organize their service delivery in some of the following ways:

- One teacher might take grades 8 and 9 while the other teacher takes Grades 10–12.
- One teacher might focus on the humanities classes while the other focuses on the science/math classes. Electives are divided between the two teachers.

- The teachers may combine either of the above options with a daily skills block and a daily tutorial block. They might both choose to be present in the skills block to directly teach the skills and strategies necessary for the skills development of those students assigned to that block (i.e., life skills, basic reading, writing and math skills, job-related skills). They might choose to have only one teacher present in the tutorial block and to use senior students as tutors.
- They might decide to co-teach a math class with a math teacher, and co-teach an English class with an English teacher.
- They might decide to alternate their focus grades so they can monitor their caseload over several years.

In all cases, the resource team would meet weekly to share their expertise, ideas, and concerns. The key, of course, to all successful teacher collaboration is that it be built on strong relationships, mutual trust, and respect. The resource teacher actively works to cultivate these relationships.

The Evolving Roles of Resource Teachers

A resource person following this non-categorical model works very closely with classroom teachers in trying to meet the needs of *all* of the students in their classrooms. Their work is influenced by the belief that collaborative planning, teaching, and assessing better addresses the diverse needs of students by creating ongoing effective programming in the classroom. It allows more students to be reached. It also focuses on the ongoing context for learning for the students, not just on specific remediation of skills, removed from the learning context of the classroom. And, finally, it builds a repertoire of strategies for classroom teachers to support the range of students in their classes when the resource teacher is not in the classroom. This collaboration is easier to manage using a non-categorical model because each resource teacher's time is devoted to fewer teachers. Instead of trying to talk and plan with every staff member, the resource teacher has a more limited number of teachers with whom to work closely.

Traditionally, resource teachers gave a battery of assessments and wrote many special programs and report cards. In this model, it is more common for resource teachers to write individual reports on classroom-based adaptations in collaboration with others. They observe students regularly and use assessment techniques that connect with the classroom. No longer are individual students routinely pulled out of the classroom as the first method of intervention.

Service Delivery as a Reflection of Inclusiveness

Non-categorical resource teachers work collaboratively with the classroom teacher to meet the teacher's and the students' needs. How they might do this is limited only by the teachers' combined creativity. The following menu describes in detail some of the roles a resource teacher might take.

Menu for Resource Teachers

Co-planning with the classroom teacher is essential in all the roles a resource teacher plays, whether service delivery is in the classroom or in the resource room. The teachers must communicate in order that a student's program be connected in meaningful ways, and that the learning goals for the student be mutually reinforced by all the adults who are working with him/her. It is imperative that the most vulnerable students have the most consistent program.

A. Co-teaching

1. The resource teacher and classroom teacher may schedule in weekly blocks of time when they teach together in the classroom. This can look many different ways:
   - The two teachers may divide the lesson, each teaching different parts. In an elementary class, one teacher might introduce a class novel or a picture book, while the other teacher models a think-aloud with the text. In a secondary class, one teacher might present information orally and visually, while the other teacher models how to take notes on the presentation using an interactive whiteboard, a projector and a computer, or an overhead projector.
   - One teacher may teach the lesson, the other taking a role that includes monitoring student behavior, scribing on the overhead or chart paper, supporting specific students, and adapting the instructions or expectations of the assignment.
   - One teacher may model a lesson for the other teacher on a current learning strategy or a graphic organizer.
   - Together, the teachers may conduct a reading or writing assessment to monitor student growth and to inform future plans for teaching.

   When two teachers are co-teaching, there are twice as many opportunities for students to receive descriptive feedback on their learning. This feedback is more likely to be personal and timely, thus having a great impact on improving learning (Black & Wiliams, 1998; Hattie & Timperley, 2008).

   At the middle and secondary levels, being visible in the classroom helps the resource teacher demystify his/her work and build relationships with more students. Then, when the resource teacher is in his/her room during a resource block, students who are not on the targeted list are more likely to come for assistance, as they already know the resource teacher.

2. The resource teacher and classroom teacher may take separate groups of students:
   - The resource teacher may take one group to work on a specific skill, such as adding to ten; the classroom teacher may take a group of students working with numbers to 100.

"One rationale for co-teaching is that when two people have planned the lesson with the group and individuals in mind, then the lesson is usually richer and the activities are adapted and modified for individual students. Both teachers then know what they are going to do and what students may need individual assistance to begin their work."

— Margaret Dixon, principal

"Every few weeks, I send an e-mail to the staff reminding them of my Learning Resource-in-the-Classroom Block(s). In general, I try to be consistently in the same classroom for about a month (or a unit). At times, there might be a block where my assistance might not be needed. By having my e-mail out there, I can head to another classroom that asked for some help whenever I was available. As a resource teacher, this keeps me busy and in many classrooms — just my goal!"

— Barb McLaughlin, resource teacher

- The class may be working on two novels, and each teacher takes one group of students.
- In a primary language arts class, both teachers may work with guided reading groups. As the students' needs change, the teacher might work with literature circles, while the resource teacher works with a group of students who need guided reading. In an intermediate, middle, or secondary English class, one teacher may read the least-challenging book in the literature circles collection and work with the students reading that book, while the other teacher works with the students reading the other book choices.
- Each teacher may take a group of students to do small-group or individual assessment.
- During the writing process, one teacher may be working with most of the class while the other conferences with individual students.

B. *Working with small groups or individual students*

Notice that the learning need determines the grouping, not the designation of the student.

1. One teacher works with a select group of students while the other teaches the whole class:
   - A small group may be working on a specific project to extend their learning.
   - A small group may need some pre-teaching of vocabulary that will be introduced in the upcoming theme/unit/chapter.
   - A small group may need some work in specific skills, such as decoding, study strategies, and note-taking.
2. One teacher works with a student, targeting the instruction to the goals outlined on this student's Individual Education Plan.
3. One teacher works with an individual or small group of students, collecting assessment data necessary to monitor student progress and to plan further intervention.

   No matter where the intervention is occurring, it has been co-planned. This co-planning is critical. It does not preclude pullout as an intervention, but the results of the pullout program **must** bridge to and show up in the classroom.

C. *Consultation*

1. In many cases, the co-planning or consultation is all that is required. Often, if the classroom teacher and resource teacher work together to co-plan a unit of study and outline ways to adapt and modify for individual students, decide on criteria, or develop assessment tools, the classroom teacher feels comfortable teaching the unit alone.
2. The resource person may conduct MAPS sessions for individual students (see chapter 11).

D. *Peer/Parent/Tutor programming*

1. Many resource teachers block out periods of time to train peer and/or parent tutors and then include the tutors in student programming. Resource teachers who have been successful in this area find they are able to meet a wider range of student needs.

E. Special Education Assistants

1. The resource teacher helps in the development of, and monitoring of, programs for the special education assistants, who give specific support to students on individual education plans.

Collaborating with the Classroom Teacher

Notice that the menu does not indicate the location of service delivery. The location is omitted purposefully because, often when teachers and resource teachers meet, the *first* item on the agenda is where the service will take place rather than what service is needed.

If the conversation focuses on the learning goals of the teacher and students, rather than on the location, the planning process changes dramatically. The question of whether the service will take place in the classroom or as a pullout program is really the last and least important question to be asked. If it's the first one, then the teachers would be obliged to figure out who they should pull out and why. Non-categorical resource teachers prefer to talk about what classroom teachers and their students need and then decide how the teachers can work together. They might very well choose to pull some kids out, with either the resource teacher or the classroom teacher teaching the class.

When teachers understand there are many options and begin to work with them, the decision of pullout versus in-class delivery becomes irrelevant. The *plan*, based on the discussion of needs, is the critical element. As our colleague Leyton Schnellert says, "No plan, no point."

We can remember the nightmare of having a full schedule of pullout programs and thirty referrals for new students sitting in our letter trays. As learning assistance teachers, we listened to our colleagues talk about their caseloads and about the stress: "How will I be able to see all these kids? What am I going to do?" "I change my schedule over and over again and still I can't see all the kids." "I don't see the kids often enough to make a difference." "I feel guilty asking the teachers to do anything more because I know they are so busy, but my students really need more time practicing what I am teaching them and that needs to happen in the classroom as follow-up."

Thirty new referrals meant that you needed to talk to teachers, observe students, assess and evaluate students, plan programs, and somehow get some children off your caseload in order to put new students on. It was the old cure mentality. We needed to cure the ones we were working with first, in order to take on new children. No wonder we worried all the time, because we managed to cure so few! We need to be more strategic and focus on increasing lifelong learning skills and helping students become more independent learners, more socially able, more collaborative, and better personal advocates.

When working as a non-categorical resource teacher in the classroom, you get to know all of the students and their classroom teachers very well. You and the classroom teacher are in constant conversation about the students, you discuss adaptations and modifications, you figure out ways to enrich the program for some students. Because you better know all of the students and the curricular expectations; because you see

"The single most important thing I can do when I co-teach in a classroom and I don't yet know the clientele well is to do a sample/demo lesson. I spend the time frontend loading some information and vocabulary so they can ALL be thinking and feel like they now know something about it before we begin a lesson. This definitely helps with belonging in a classroom."

— Kim Boettcher

them doing daily work; because you are in the classroom watching them struggle with writing, make inappropriate comments during carpet time, lose focus or disengage, or rise to a challenge; you are doing formative assessment all the time. You and the classroom teacher now discuss what is happening for individual students in the classroom's learning context more comfortably. Adaptations are made with much more ease because you know the context, the academic and social environment, and the student. Rarely now are you asked to "assess" a child the way you used to, using a standardized battery of tests. And when you are, you are not canceling your pullout groups to do it, but seamlessly assessing during your scheduled classroom time.

You find that referral forms are no longer needed because you know the children and are continually problem-solving. You no longer feel like you are totally responsible for "saving" children who previously were names on a referral form. True collaboration is an incredible stress reducer, as you and your colleagues share the load and witness the difference your collaboration makes to learners.

Of course, no referral forms does not imply that there is no paper work to be done. Individual Education Plans remain essential, but many resource teachers have found that the nature of the IEP changes dramatically due to the shift in service delivery. The IEP, now classroom-based, is a living document that the resource teacher, the classroom teacher, and the special education assistant can use *daily* to support learning.

Making the Service Delivery Menu Work

When teachers see there is a menu of choices, their thinking on how to best work with a resource person often changes. Many classroom teachers have experienced working with special education or ESL resource people in only one way — pullout programs where the resource person does something to "fix" the student. If you ask classroom teachers what they want or need, many will still respond by saying, "I'd like you to assess and work with these three or six or ten kids," because this is all they have known.

Resource teachers may wish to structure their first meeting with a classroom teacher in such a way that it takes the focus off individual students and puts it on the teacher, the class, and the goals for the class. Individual learning needs are then addressed, starting within the context of that classroom environment rather than as an add-on. Alternatively, the classroom teacher may be the catalyst for change by requesting a different type of service from a resource person who has traditionally offered only one way of service delivery. Classroom teachers may want to consider the questions that appear in Checklist for Assessing the Nature of Service Delivery, on page 107.

Basic prerequisites to successful collaboration are trust, flexibility, and good communication skills. For two people to work closely together, share their needs safely with each other, teach in front of each other, and

Checklist for Assessing the Nature of Service Delivery

The classroom teacher is ultimately responsible for the educational programming of the students in his or her classroom. Bearing this in mind, review the following questions:

1. Can you account for or explain what is happening to support the students' learning while they are out of the room with a specialist (teacher, counselor, etc.)?

2. Is the program set up by the specialist in concert with the learning program of your classroom and of the designated student?

3. Were you part of the planning of the program and the decision of where service delivery takes place?

4. Have you ever questioned where service delivery is taking place?

5. Have you invited your learning assistance teacher, your ESL teacher, or a reading teacher into the classroom to work with your students in collaboration with you?

6. Do you think there is a transfer of what is being taught outside the classroom to work situations inside your classroom?

7. Are the students becoming more independent as learners as a result of your combined efforts?

Pembroke Publishers © 2011 *Learning in Safe Schools, revised edition* by Faye Brownlie and Judith King ISBN 978-1-55138-266-1

make plans work, they must feel confident that what takes place in the classroom may be celebrated elsewhere but is not critiqued elsewhere.

There are a variety of ways for the resource teacher to make a timetable. Some of them are outlined below. See a sample elementary timetable on page 112 and a sample middle/secondary timetable on page 113.

Build a collaborative timetable

One resource teacher we know calls together the classroom teachers she is working with. They briefly describe their needs and wishes, then all of them make up the timetable. The resource teacher leads the discussion and speaks about the varying needs in the classrooms, but lets the teachers make most of the decisions. She has found over time that, for the most part, the teachers are very responsive to each other's needs. Teachers may not have their wishes met, but they understand why this is so, are more aware of the bigger picture, and have taken part in the decision-making process.

Create flexible timetables

Many resource teachers make up flexible timetables. They put a schedule in place for a period of time, such as a six-week period or from October to December. They may spend more time with a few teachers or focusing on development of a specific skill in this period, and then switch to spending more time with a different few in January.

Administer school-wide or grade-wide performance-based reading assessments to guide instruction

In some elementary schools, the second week of September is reading assessment week. All the students from K–7 work with a whole-class performance-based reading assessment that is organized by the resource team. Classroom teachers sign up for the two periods (generally running between forty-five and sixty minutes) they would like to use to administer the assessment. Resource teachers, administration, librarians, and other non-enrolling staff join the classroom teacher, so no teacher is administering the assessment alone. In some cases, the resource teacher leads the assessment; in others, the classroom teacher does. All participating staff follow the common protocol, listen to students read, and interview the students about their reading. At the completion of the assessment, all information is collected — the running record, the interview, the student's response paper. At a convenient time, such as a professional development day, all staff meet to code the assessments in teams and design class or grade action plans, based on the strengths and needs shown by applying the performance standards. This information is shared with the staff so all know one another's goals and plans. The assessment is repeated within a six- to eight-week period, goals are monitored, and new goals are established.

At middle or secondary school, the resource team, sometimes in conjunction with the literacy team, chooses a common class period or a common subject for all incoming students to participate in the reading assessment. A similar pattern is followed: the resource and literacy teams help administer the assessment; no teacher assesses or codes alone; goals and plans are made and shared with the entire staff, based on the results of the formative assessment. The resource team can then help design appropriate strategies for different subject areas to assist teachers in developing specific skills, common across the grade, with their students. At the middle and secondary level, it is more common for subsequent formative assessments to be conducted in individual teachers' classrooms, often with resource support. A summative assessment at the end of the year or the end of the semester must be of a parallel, performance-based format in order to gauge whether the teaching is making a difference. (For more information on designing and using these kinds of assessments, see Brownlie and Schnellert, 2009; Brownlie, Feniak and Schnellert, 2006; or http://insinc.com/ministryofeducation/20041007/archive.html).

Prioritize needs and wishes

Some resource teachers invite the teachers they are responsible for to give them their classroom timetables marked with the periods they wish the resource teacher would be available to work with them. They prioritize the areas by color or number. The resource teacher then works with the timetables like a jigsaw puzzle, trying to meet as many high-priority needs as possible.

Develop mini-units based on staff need

In one school, the intermediate staff decided they needed to work with students on study strategies. Instead of each intermediate teacher developing the strategies, they brainstormed for the most important ideas and developed an outline together. The resource teacher then co-taught the unit with each classroom teacher, adapting and changing the unit based on the experiences she was having in each classroom. At the end of the unit, the teachers had developed a mini-course that each of them could then use every year in their classrooms.

In a similar instance, a resource teacher and a classroom teacher developed a number of lessons to introduce and use during buddy reading in the classroom. The resource teacher and classroom teacher then offered to work with any teacher in the school who also wanted to use the unit.

Resource teachers who do this on a regular basis generally block out a period of time each week and offer that period on a rotating basis to anyone on staff. This type of service delivery needs to be discussed and agreed to by the staff as a whole.

Co-plan

Especially at the middle and secondary levels, some resource teachers save a period to co-plan with teachers. At this time, if they are not meeting together and co-planning, the resource teacher collects materials, creates assignments or assessment rubrics, and creates adapted or modified material, assignments, or assessments. Resource teachers are also available at this time to go into different classes and monitor how their materials, assignments, and adaptations are working. They might also get a heads-up from the teacher on their next unit, so students in the resource block can be introduced to key vocabulary and graphic organizers, and appropriate background knowledge can be built.

Holding the Resource Team Model Up to the Light

Resource teachers need to be actively involved with students and teachers in September. However, some resource teachers spend September (and even October) assessing at-risk and ESL students and doing IEPs, and then canceling programs again in January and June to update IEPs or to reassess. When resource teams choose to do this they communicate negative messages:

- that effective programming cannot happen in the classroom until their particular assessments have been completed;
- that paper work is more important than working with students and teachers;
- that identification of students "to get more money" is the ultimate goal, secondary to making real changes for those students; and
- that intervention cannot happen for students with special needs until an IEP is written.

Working with teachers and students to make changes for students in a visible, collaborative way, on a regular basis, is the highest priority — and needs to come first. Classroom teachers have a great deal of paper work to do, especially around report card time. Resource teachers have a great deal of paper work to do throughout the year. Both classroom teachers and resource teachers do need time to talk and plan and write IEPs together. However, it is detrimental to the image of the team, and to service delivery for students, when resource teams cancel programs to do their paper work.

Often, in September, it is not possible to write up a timetable for resource teachers such as those on pages 112 and 113. Class reviews have not taken place, needs have not been established, and teacher timetables are in flux. September is a great month for resource teachers to be in classrooms, getting to know teachers and their new students. During this time there are many options for them, including these:

- observing individual students who had been identified the previous year;
- assisting in the transition for some students moving from one teacher to another;
- modifying behavior programs for students so that the transition is more easily made;

- working closely with classroom teachers receiving students who need major adaptations or modifications so that the teacher can assist the student from the start;
- modeling strategies that worked for particular students;
- working side-by-side in the classroom with the teacher, getting to know the style of the teacher, the expectations of the teacher, the triggers of the teacher, the classroom context and its various social groupings; and
- teaching the whole class while the teacher gets to know students individually.

More permanent schedules can begin to form after class reviews have taken place and the resource teachers have been in the classes, working with and getting to know students, and listening to teachers' needs.

Reflecting on the Value of the Non-categorical Resource Teacher Model

When staff in a school "walk the talk" of collaboration, a model is set for students. Students no longer see an "expert" model where students are whisked down the hall for "special" programs. Rather they see ongoing decision-making and problem-solving as professionals employ the best of their practice to create positive learning environments for all students. Students see teachers reflecting alone and together on their practice. They learn to respect differences and to employ the social aspects of learning. Since labeling and pullout programs are less common, students are not set up by their differences or the places where they receive their programming. Belonging in the classroom increases their feelings of security and hence, the ability to learn (Kim Schonert-Reichl, 2006).

**Sample Elementary Day, Non-categorical
Resource Teacher Timetable**

8:15–8:45	School-based team meeting
8:45–9:30	Grade 6/7 Literature Circles: The resource teacher and the classroom teacher each meet with a group of students who are reading a common book while other students are writing their responses or reading.
9:30–10:15	Grade 1/2 Guided Reading: Class is divided into four homogeneous reading groups. Each teacher takes two groups and works with one group while the other group reads silently for about 20 minutes. Groups are redefined and moved between the teachers every six weeks.
10:15–10:30	Recess
10:30–11:15	Grade 2/3 Math: Provide support in the math classroom and, when needed, take out a small group for review and/or further instruction.
11:15–12:00	Grade 3/4 Writing: Since the classroom teacher is new to this grade level, often the resource teacher introduces new writing strategies. At other times, they co-teach and conference with the students.
12:00–12:50	LUNCH
12:50–1:35	Kindergarten Writing Co-teaching: This happens three times/week. Together, with student input, the teachers draw a picture, write labels and simple sentences on chart paper. All students date their page and use pictures and their writing to tell a story. One work table (out of five) becomes the quiet table, where one teacher works and supports those students. The other teacher circulates and supports the remaining students.
1:35–2:20	Grade 6/7 (same class as the morning): Focus on individuals needing additional support. Some small-group skills-focused pullout in math, reading, or writing, on a needs basis, especially focusing on new ESL learners. These needs may be common or not. Monitor the work created by the resource teacher for a student with significant cognitive delays; this work is completed when the student cannot work with the class. However, the classroom teacher has become increasingly adept at including this student, having him draw a picture after a science experiment, act as class photographer when students are working on experiments or projects.
2:20–3:00	DPA (daily physical activity): Either participate or use this time for paperwork.

Sample Middle/Secondary Non-categorical Resource Teacher Timetable, Semestered School

8:40–9:45   Resource Room: The Resource Room is open all day and is always staffed by a resource teacher, an educational assistant, and at least one Grade 11 or 12 peer tutor. A maximum of seventeen students have this block in their timetable (typically high-incidence students or students who need additional monitoring and support). Other students can drop in for assistance. Students check in at the beginning of the class and establish personal goals for the day. Mini-lessons are conducted partway through the block, based on student goals — using scientific calculators, balancing equations, planning an essay, integrating quotations into their writing. Students report out at the end of the class: what needs to be completed for homework, something they want help with in the next class. The goal-setting helps the resource teacher see when he/she needs to touch base with a subject area teacher and builds community.

9:45–10:15   BREAK

10:15–11:35   Support Block: This block is available for co-teaching with teachers with whom the resource teacher collaborates. Sometimes the block is divided in half so two classes can be attended to. New classes are chosen on a monthly basis. On days when it is known that the resource teacher will not be needed, an e-mail alerts other teachers on his/her caseload that he/she is available for support in the classroom.

11:35–11:55   Uninterrupted Silent Reading, school-wide: Attend different classes to read. Ensure that targeted students have an appropriate text with them.

11:55–12:38   LUNCH

12:38–1:53   Skills Block (for students with low-incidence funding): Five or six students per block, with an educational assistant present as well. Skills focus on life skills, toileting, basic literacy and numeracy, individual social and behavioral goals, building a sense of community and belonging.

1:53–2:00   BREAK

2:00–3:15   Co-teaching Science 10 (every second day, alternating with Math 8): These classes have been chosen because data indicated that more students were found vulnerable in these content areas at these grades than in others. Co-plan, co-teach, and co-assess with one classroom teacher who also teaches at least one other block of Science 10 or Math 8 on their own.

10

Implementing Class Reviews

With thanks to Donna Webb, Claire Joyce, Joyce Tait, Shelley Moore, Catriona Misfeldt, Leyton Schnellert, and Jeri Jacovac

School-based teams play a crucial role in developing safe and inclusive schools. They make many decisions about children's lives, and their language influences teachers, parents, and students. If school-based teams have tunnel vision, speak categorically, or use judgmental language, then everyone in the school is affected in subtle or nonsubtle ways.

Most school-based teams set in place processes for dealing with issues, whether whole-school, classroom, or individual issues. Some of these processes work better than others in promoting open communication, collaboration, and a real and optimistic sense of problem-solving.

It is common practice in many schools in the fall of the year to invite teachers to meet with members of the school-based team and share information about their students. We believe this is an important structure. Over the past years, we have added elements to this structure that support our vision of inclusive schools. We have found it beneficial to begin classroom reviews by focusing on the class as a whole (strengths and needs) and on the teacher's goals. In this way we gain the big picture of the classroom, so that when we discuss the individual needs of students, we can do it in context of the classroom.

"I consider the class review process to be a form of social justice."

— Dan Kalynchuk, middle school principal

The Class Review Structure: Elementary, Middle, and Secondary

1. Allow 45–60 minutes for each class review.

2. All members of the school-based team attend; this includes principal and/or vice principal, resource/learning assistance, ESL teachers, counselors, plus the classroom teacher and educational assistant, if there is one working in the classroom. At the secondary level, the meeting might include only the class teacher, the resource teacher, the counselor, and/or the special education assistant or educational assistant.

3. Speech and language clinicians and district support staff, such as members of the autism team and Aboriginal Support workers, attend as they are able, when it is known in advance that the needs of the class might involve them, or if it is already known that they will be working with students in the class.

4. The review occurs during class time. A teacher-on-call (substitute teacher) is provided for the classroom teacher.

5. The classroom teacher is given a set of questions before the meeting that she/he will be asked to respond to at the meeting (see A Framework for Class Review: The Classroom Teacher's Perspective on page 116). Some teachers choose to record their responses to these questions in advance, but many simply use the questions to help organize their thinking. It is an advance organizer for the conversation.

6. One of the members of the school-based team facilitates the conversation, posing the questions in order, clarifying, and seeking examples. The questions asked in order are:
   1. What are the strengths of your class as a whole?
   2. What are the needs of your class as a whole?
   3. What are your goals for the class as a whole?

7. A second member of the school-based team records the conversation on the form (page 117).

8. The classroom teacher is the main speaker, not the facilitator nor the recorder. Members of the school-based team add any information they have about individual members of the class (see question 4 in the Framework for Class Review on page 116) once the classroom teacher has responded to the three whole-class questions.

9. The final question, "What decisions can be made?" is critical. Tentative decisions might be made after the classroom teacher has described the classroom strengths and needs, and his/her goals, and once the individual concerns have been addressed. Many schools choose to arrange a further meeting (a *what's next* meeting) for the classroom teacher and the specific resource teacher to build a plan for how they are going to work together.

   It is important to always keep in mind that these meetings are meant to be action-oriented. The support teachers/principal and/or vice principal are looking at ways to support the classroom teacher in meeting the goals for the students in the classroom. For example, a resource teacher might offer to share some resources at the initial meeting, or later follow through on suggestions made to address the classroom teacher's goals; the principal may agree to set up a meeting with a parent. In the *what's next* meeting, the staff involved meets to make a more thorough plan. These meetings are scheduled for a week after class reviews.

10. Class Reviews are not IEP meetings. The focus is on the whole class — their strengths, their needs, their interactions, and how individual students can learn and grow within this classroom context.

A Framework for Class Review:
The Classroom Teacher's Perspective

1. What are the strengths of the class? What are the positive things about this group as a whole?

2. What are your concerns about the class as a whole? What are their needs? What do you wonder about?

3. What are your main goals this year?
   (These goals may be based on strengths and/or concerns, or on an area of interest, or on a new grade level or curriculum. Each teacher may have three or four.)

4. What are the individual needs (medical, learning, social-emotional, language, or other related to individual students) in your classroom?

Pembroke Publishers © 2011 *Learning in Safe Schools, revised edition* by Faye Brownlie and Judith King ISBN 978-1-55138-266-1

Class Review Recording Form

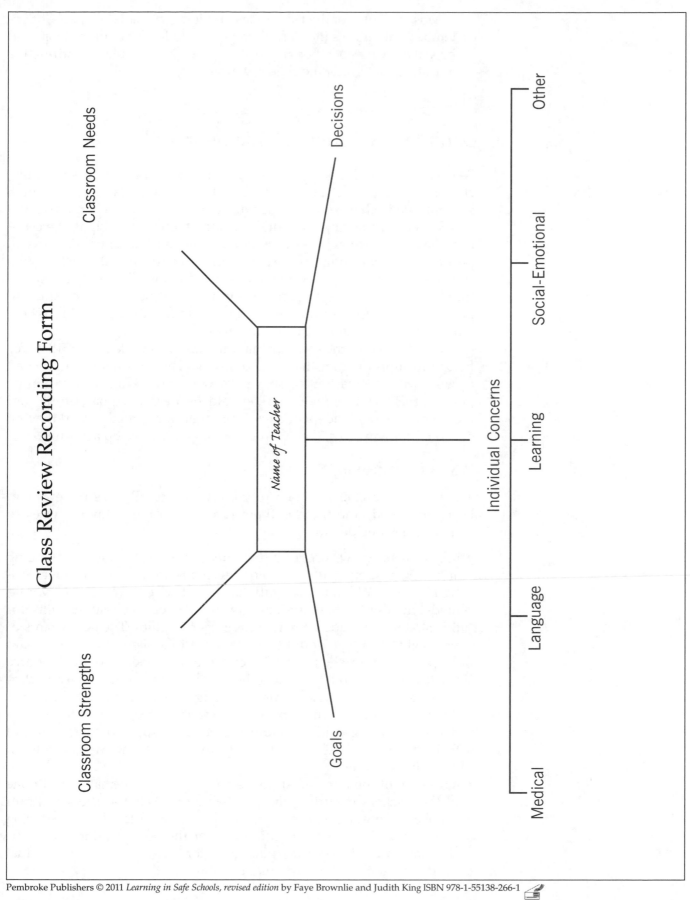

Classroom Strengths

Classroom Needs

Name of Teacher

Decisions

Goals

Individual Concerns

Medical

Language

Learning

Social-Emotional

Other

Pembroke Publishers © 2011 *Learning in Safe Schools, revised edition* by Faye Brownlie and Judith King ISBN 978-1-55138-266-1

Most schools conduct their class reviews in the latter half of September. This allows the classroom teacher to learn about the class and how they work together. She or he is then better able to address the questions that guide the class review.

Sample Class Review: Elementary

See Class Profile/Review on page 119 for an example of a 45-minute, class review meeting about a combined Grade 4/5 class. The Grade 5 students are in their second year with the classroom teacher. Present at this September meeting were the principal, the vice-principal, the classroom teacher, all members of the resource team (this school has several part-time non-enrolling support teachers), an educational assistant who supported the teacher the previous year and knows the teacher and half the class, the itinerant school counselor, and the itinerant speech and language clinician. One of the resource teachers facilitated the discussion, while the vice-principal filled in the form.

It was decided at the meeting that this class was a likely candidate for first-term support from the area counselor. The counselor volunteered to work with the teacher for six weeks, once a week for a forty-minute period. The focus of their work would be personal goal-setting and increasing personal independence. The counselor agreed to lead the first session. Following this, they would co-plan for follow-up activities.

What's Next Meeting

The resource teacher assigned to the class (once all class reviews had been completed) and the classroom teacher met the following week to co-plan. They decided to

- begin a reading/writing unit (for three weeks) focusing on belonging and social responsibility. Based on this focus, they chose the novel *Shabash* by Anne Walsh to use with the class. The resource teacher would model the think-aloud strategy, gradually releasing responsibility for this strategy to students reading together in pairs. The "quadrants of a thought" strategy would be introduced to assist with focusing and deepening comprehension. The classroom teacher and the resource teacher would model this together. The social responsibility performance standards would be used to judge the characters' behavior in the novel. Students would be asked to write in response to these standards, providing evidence from the novel to support their rating of their chosen character's behavior. The resource teacher would co-teach three times a week.
- have each of the targeted students engage in a conversation with one of the teachers regarding the text being read. Due to the significant number of language concerns in the class, this would take place during co-teaching times. The specific focus of the conversation would be determined by the class learning goals for the day and the individual needs and goals of the particular student.

Class Review Recording Form

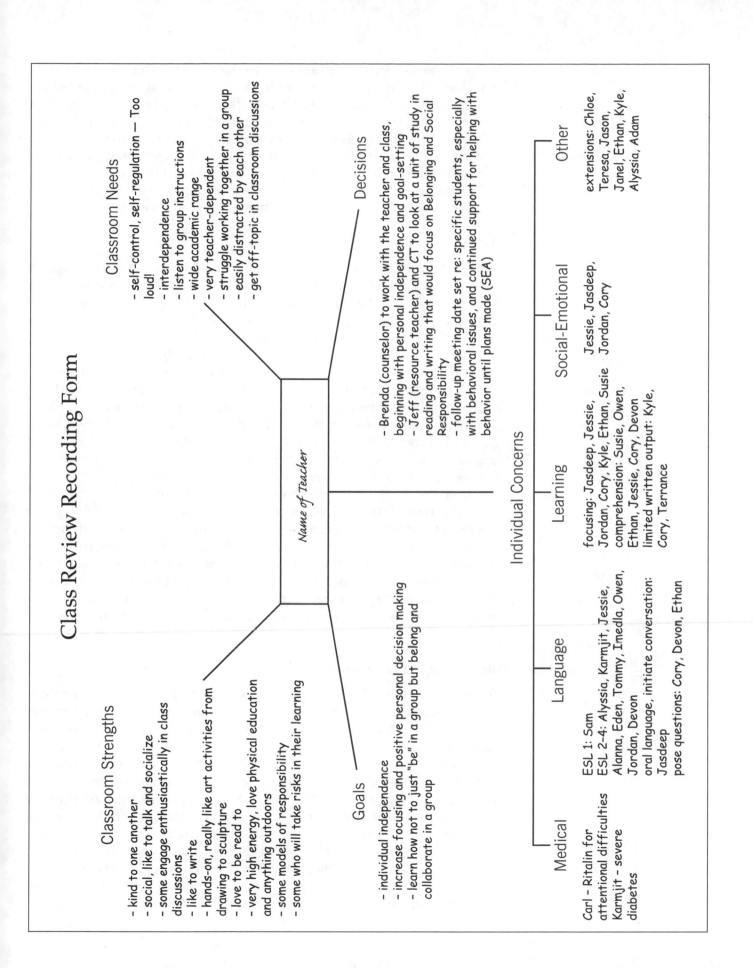

Name of Teacher

Classroom Strengths

- kind to one another
- social, like to talk and socialize
- some engage enthusiastically in class discussions
- like to write
- hands-on, really like art activities from drawing to sculpture
- love to be read to
- very high energy, love physical education and anything outdoors
- some models of responsibility
- some who will take risks in their learning

Classroom Needs

- self-control, self-regulation — Too loud!
- interdependence
- listen to group instructions
- wide academic range
- very teacher-dependent
- struggle working together in a group
- easily distracted by each other
- get off-topic in classroom discussions

Goals

- individual independence
- increase focusing and positive personal decision making
- learn how not to just "be" in a group but belong and collaborate in a group

Decisions

- Brenda (counselor) to work with the teacher and class, beginning with personal independence and goal-setting
- Jeff (resource teacher) and CT to look at a unit of study in reading and writing that would focus on Belonging and Social Responsibility
- follow-up meeting date set re: specific students, especially with behavioral issues, and continued support for helping with behavior until plans made (SEA)

Individual Concerns

Medical	Language	Learning	Social-Emotional	Other
Carl – Ritalin for attentional difficulties *Karmjit* – severe diabetes	ESL 1: Sam ESL 2–4: Alyssia, Karmjit, Jessie, Alanna, Eden, Tommy, Imedla, Owen, Jordan, Devon oral language, initiate conversation: Jasdeep pose questions: Cory, Devon, Ethan	focusing: Jasdeep, Jessie, Jordan, *Cory*, Kyle, Ethan, Susie comprehension: Susie, Owen, Ethan, Jessie, Cory, Devon limited written output: Kyle, Cory, Terrance	Jessie, Jasdeep, Jordan, Cory	extensions: Chloe, Teresa, Jason, Janel, Ethan, Kyle, Alyssia, Adam

- use more descriptive feedback and co-created criteria for all assignments
- include the educational assistant in the planning of appropriate behavioral goals for four students: Jessie, Jasdeep, Jordan, and Cory. The educational assistant was assigned to the class for much of the day, particularly during key academic times — language arts, math, science, and social studies — largely due to health and safety issues as a result of the behavioral challenges of Jessie, Jasdeep, Jordan, and Cory. Her task was to work alongside the teacher, helping the students reach their behavioral goals and providing support as necessary.

Time Allocations

Schools that use the class review process find that it makes sense to assign their resource allocation to classes after the reviews have been held. The philosophy is that fair is not equal. Until the school-based team has a complete picture of the needs of the classes of the school, time allocation of specific resources cannot be made.

What this means to teachers is that no one teacher is going to be left with "that class." If the needs of a particular class are evident to the team, then the team attempts to increase their resource time or perhaps the time of a special education assistant in the class, and to decrease the time in a less-needy class, based on the relative needs of the school. This models an "all in this together" approach. From the perspective of the resource teachers and the principal, the decisions have been made by a team as a school decision to best address the needs of the school population, and not from the more limited perspective of an individual.

In the two or three weeks prior to the class review meetings, the resource team makes a schedule of support for the students with health and safety concerns, creates temporary schedules for the paraprofessionals, and spends time working in classes with the classroom teachers to better understand the nature of the new groups of students and how the students with special needs are fitting in. Then they, too, at the class review meetings, have a more detailed understanding of the school's classes.

Revisiting the Class Review

Some school-based teams offer classroom teachers the option of meeting with the team to revisit their class review in January. This gives everyone a chance to work together to review successes and challenges and to set new directions and goals.

In some schools, where the student population is very stable, schools have adapted the class review process and conduct class reviews in June to review the successes of the year and to prepare for the next year. In June, the next year's teacher is invited to join the conversation that is being led by the current teacher. This gives a heads-up for planning for the beginning of the school year and is followed up with another class review in September. In other schools with stable populations, the previous year's teacher is asked to join the class review in September, as he or she can bring a wealth of information to the conversation.

With thanks to Deborah Ralston and the staff at Cayoosh Elementary

There are many ways for this process to play out. At Cayoosh Elementary School, a small rural school in Lillooet, BC, the class reviews are held in September and are updated in January and late May. They are created and displayed on an interactive whiteboard. Each time a review is held, the recording is done in a different color. Everyone can easily see what changes are being made, celebrate the growth, and witness the power of collaboration — different people seeing different strengths in different students. The secondary team (academic counselor, principal, resource teacher, Aboriginal Student Support Worker) is invited to the May class review update meeting. The focused conversation extends to include the incoming group of educators.

Class Reviews: Middle and Secondary

In middle schools, the class review is held with several classroom teachers present; teachers who teach the same cohort of students all attend. Because these teachers will be sharing the same cohort of students for the year, there is much to be learned by all four of them addressing the same questions, examining the students through the lens of their content. When decisions are being made, the team of teachers and the resource teacher work together for support in co-creating the schedule.

Often in secondary schools, one teacher (not just an English teacher or a core academic area teacher, but any teacher who wishes to engage in a conversation about how to better meet the needs in his or her class) chooses to accept the invitation to meet with specific members of a school-based team — perhaps a resource teacher for that grade or that subject area, a counselor, and a paraprofessional. The meeting follows a similar format, with the teacher leading the conversation and others filling in. Action plans are created before the meeting ends. Guiding questions for this conversation include

- How will we work together to support the needs of the students in your class?
- What challenges do you have in teaching your curriculum to this diverse group of students that I can help with?
- What strategies do you currently use to address diversity in your class?"

Sample Class Review: Grade 9 Social Studies

A Grade 9 social studies teacher, the resource teacher, and an educational assistant meet for their class review meeting. The classroom teacher has filled in his form in advance. He talks his way through his notes, describing the class overall as being quiet, orderly, intent on doing their homework and getting the right answers. He is concerned that they are not taking risks with their thinking, exploring options, or defending their opinions. At this point they do not work well in groups, though they are polite to one another. He wants them to experience the power of working together, to think more deeply, to not worry so much about a right answer but to consider different perspectives, and to be able to support these perspectives. His over-arching question for the year is this: How does the evolution of society help meet society's needs?

The resource teacher and the educational assistant (EA) share their information about individual students. There are two students with low-incidence designation (one has developmental delays; the other has autism, significant challenges with transitions, and some perseverating behavior), three students with high-incidence designations (learning disabilities, gifted), others with non-designated concerns (written-output challenges, an elective mute, severely withdrawn, flight risk), and ten students who are learning English as an additional language. In addition, from past experience with many of these students, they know that organization of ideas and time on long-term projects is a challenge.

The team decides that, in order to best address the needs of this class, they will meet again and do some co-planning. The social studies teacher will come prepared with the learning outcomes he wants to address in his upcoming unit. He will also bring the materials he has used in the past and will be prepared to discuss strategies he finds effective in dealing with the class.

What's Next Meeting
At the planning meeting (of the social studies teacher, EA, and resource teacher) the following decisions are made:

- The resource teacher suggests that they focus on interactive small-group strategies to address the goals of deeper learning, moving beyond one right answer, and working with others. The resource teacher suggests they might consider co-teaching to implement the interactive strategies. Co-teaching is not a common practice in the school at this point.
- Given the diversity of needs in the class, the resource teacher volunteers to design pre-reading activities to help build background knowledge (may help with risk-taking), graphic organizers (for note-taking, organizing information, seeing relationships), and alternative ways to demonstrate understanding. As well, the resource teacher will prepare parallel materials (simple texts, response activities, picture books) for the EA to use to teach students who are working more than two years below grade level, and for whom teaching and time are unlikely to close the gap. The EA will be working within the class with the targeted students, but will also be available to work on short-term interventions with other students
- They agree that the more the teacher explains the learning outcomes he expects in his class, the more the resource teacher and the educational assistant can equip themselves with ways to support the range of students in meeting these expectations. The focus will be on the outcome, not on the time it takes to achieve this outcome or on the length of the assignment; e.g., if the outcome can be achieved in five statements and a visual, then a student with a written-output challenge would not have to write three paragraphs.
- They agree that they are likely to learn a lot from each other by co-teaching, as their expertise is quite different. In each co-taught lesson, either the social studies teacher or the resource teacher will take the

lead. They also agree to evaluate the impact of their efforts after the first unit.

Sample Class Review: Grade 8 Industrial Education

The Industrial Education teacher, the resource teacher, the counselor, and the special education assistant meet at the request of the Industrial Education teacher. He has responded to the invitation from the school-based team to meet and discuss a challenging class. The IE teacher is concerned because one particular Grade 8 IE class is particularly hard to handle. He is worried about safety issues in the workplace. After completing the class review, the IE teacher and the resource teacher decide it would be helpful if the resource teacher observes the class.

What's Next Meeting
The resource teacher recognizes that many students are having difficulty maintaining focus during the lecture on how to be safe while working with the equipment. Also, by listening to several of the students read the health and safety manual, she realizes that many of the students cannot decode the text and therefore can not understand the content.

After the class, the IE teacher, the resource teacher, and the special education assistant sit down together and design a series of three lessons that will use connecting strategies to build background knowledge and processing strategies to lend support in comprehending the text. They focus on three specific strategies: sort and predict for building vocabulary; an anticipation guide to access background knowledge and to focus reading; and a think-aloud to make explicit strategies used by expert readers (the IE teacher and the resource teacher modeling together) when reading to understand.

The resource teacher joins the IE teacher to co-teach the next three classes. The special education assistant also joins the team for these classes. In subsequent units, she will join the class to support the learning after the lessons have been co-designed, using the same strategies, by the resource teacher and the classroom teacher.

Class Review Implementation: Secondary

With thanks to Tammy Mitchell and the team at Murdoch MacKay Collegiate

River East Transcona School Division (RETSD), a suburban school division in Winnipeg, Manitoba, has noticed a significant change in their student populations as a result of a move to inclusion, changes in immigration policies, and globalization. They have been working together to develop a class review process with their secondary schools to better meet the needs of all students. They use the class review process to determine the allocation of school supports, including co-teaching or team teaching partnerships, the teaching of mini-lessons, the allocation of technology (specialized software and devices), the assignment of educational assistants, and referrals to divisional and community supports.

The implementation of class reviews started slowly at Murdoch MacKay Collegiate. District conversations that focused on ways to support student diversity and teach so all could learn began in 2004. These conversations included in-depth work on class reviews, on creating content-based literacy assessments, and on working together to use this information to inform instruction. The school began a focused implementation in 2005. Once a foundation was built with willing teachers and principal/vice principal support, the process grew. Resource teachers and counselors concentrated their support on using the collected data to inform classroom instruction, and were sure to follow through on discussed plans.

In 2011, Murdoch Mackay profiled all their Grade 9 classes and some Grade 10 classes. The process had evolved to look like this:

Week 1/First Week of September

The resource teachers distribute an information letter to all Grade 9 staff to prepare them for their class review meeting. Included with this letter are A Framework for Class Review (page 116) and the Class Profile/Review template (see below an example of a completed template). Note that the categories for individual students have been changed on the profile/review sheet to match the division's categories.

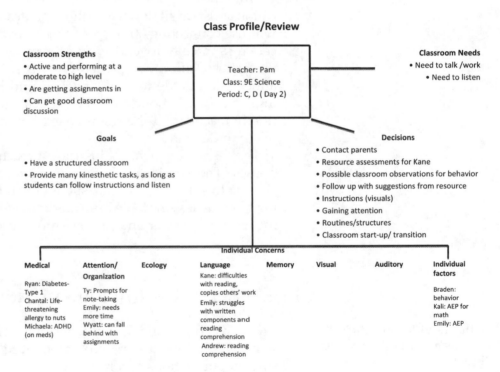

Classroom teachers (Grade 9 core content teachers) complete an informal assessment of their classes, including

- A "cold" read
- For some teachers, a classroom content-based reading assessment called the Standard Reading Assessment (see Brownlie, Feniak and Schnellert, 2006)
- A copy of a letter they have written (any letter that isn't a text message)

- A letter written to the teacher that includes this basic information:
  - family demographics
  - employment
  - personal accomplishments
  - goals for the year
  - favorite books (or not)
  - museums they have been to
  - where they will be when they graduate

Week 2

- Classroom teachers complete the Class Profile/Review sheet (see pages 119 and 124 for examples of a completed Class Profile/Review sheet) and use the Framework for Class Review (page 116) to guide them in the process.
- Teachers are encouraged to complete the top portion of the Class Profile/Review sheet with the whole class as a group.
- The resource teachers meet with classroom teachers from the core subject areas. They use the Class Profile/Review sheet to guide their discussion. They identify co-teaching opportunities and the supports required to address student specific learning and behavioral needs and to meet goals for the class. Resource teachers begin immediately to work with students who require specific learning and behavior plans.
- The resource teachers then meet with the teachers of the optional and vocational courses to share the information they have gathered and to enhance the profiles.
- The school uses teacher preparation time and "floating" substitutes to facilitate the class review process, which takes about one hour per teacher.

Six Weeks Later/Mid-October

The resource teachers meet with classroom teachers to review and revise the Class Profile/Review. They consider these questions: What is working? What is not? What do we do next?

Eight Weeks Later/End of October

- Co-teaching and/or team teaching begins.
- The resource teachers use the information gathered from the class reviews to create their schedules for the semester.
- The resource teachers move up with students from year to year; this gives them the opportunity to build on the strengths of the group of students as they progress through the grades.

A resource teacher, a counselor, and a principal/vice principal all participate in the class review process with the classroom teacher. The teacher provides valuable information about his or her assessment of the class using his or her observations of the students, conversations with the students, and student products. The resource teacher, counselor, and principal/vice principal bring supporting information to the discussion by adding data from the students' histories and pupil files. If the classroom teacher is new to teaching a particular course, the subject-area department head joins the team to be available to assist the teacher with curricular implementation.

Staff at Murdoch have embraced the process of class reviews. The sense of team and collaboration is key. They feel that they are able to meet the learning and behavioral needs of more students as they work together to use the information gathered to inform their instructional practices. More Grade 10 teachers are becoming involved. Teachers are finding they are able to adjust the requirements for students to show evidence of learning based on their strengths and areas of concern. One teacher found, upon completing the class review, that eight of the students enrolled were repeating the course. She changed her plan to accommodate the unique needs of that group of students. In addition to the co-teaching that has occurred with resource teachers, teachers have liaised with one another to team teach when an area of concern in one class fits with a strength in another. The staff have seen changes in student attendance, engagement, and success. This process is valued by school staff and has become part of the essence of their operations.

Some Cautionary Notes

- When you use this process of class reviews, insist on beginning the conversation with strengths and sticking with strengths for more than just a moment. If you are the facilitator of the class review process, probe to develop a significant list of strengths to be used in subsequent planning. This focus on strengths is particularly important in reframing thinking into more of a "can do" stance. Instead of describing a class as "constantly talking," which is not a strength, describe it as "very verbal," which is a strength, and you will notice immediately how everyone views the class differently. Instead of "this class is chaotic and constantly moving," reframe the description as "very active." Again, a different, more positive, picture is created. Too often, in the past, the class review meeting has focused on negativity and has left teachers with a feeling of gloom and doom — "Oh, there were even more challenges than I thought!" We firmly believe that starting with the positive changes the tone of the meeting and creates a positive mindset open to growth. These students are going to be together with each other and the teacher for a year or a semester. We need a positive outlook.

- Speak to the strengths, needs, and goals of the class before moving to the individual students. Spend most of your time on this first section. If classroom teachers have difficulty finding strengths, prompt them. No matter who the students of concern are, each student is a member of the classroom community, and whole-class plans need to be constructed — plans that include all the students, honoring their individual strength and needs, and the teacher's goals, within the context of the classroom. This community-first view (planning with all students in mind) is also important when designing curriculum units.

- We have addressed individual concerns in two different ways; both can be successful. One way is to begin with the class list. Call out each name on the list and invite everyone at the table to share their knowledge of this student. Include all students. Do not spend inordinate amounts of time on those students who have IEPs, as they will be discussed at a different time.

  Another way is to follow the Individual Concerns headings and ask the teacher to refer to his or her class lists after mentioning the names that come forth. It is a way to get a perspective on priorities/ needs, as teachers mention the names of the students that stand out to them, then look back at the class list and are reminded of others — "Oh yeah, I forgot about..." After the teacher has moved through his or her priorities/needs, others at the table add their information. The challenge here is to ensure that no students are overlooked in the discussion.

- Consistently try to move the language away from labels to addressing behaviors; i.e., from "autistic" to "has a difficult time transitioning from one class to another, so needs advance warning and time to prepare himself; tends to wander into a world of his own, but can be reconnected with a comment made when you are in close proximity."

11

MAPS: Planning for Individual Students

"The concept of difference should not be scary. Clearly, people are different. The concept of difference is only scary when put into a hierarchy."

— David Hingsburger, educational consultant

Planning for some students is more complex than it is for others. When a teacher, parent, or student is not satisfied with what is happening for the student in the classroom, it becomes necessary to align their goals with the school goals. To accomplish this, some schools pull together the key people in the student's life to set reasonable and consistent goals and plan a cohesive program, understood by each person who deals with the child. Such a problem-solving session happens because the child, teacher, or parent needs a more in-depth planning process. Regardless of who initiates the process, the child's needs remain paramount throughout.

A planning model called MAPS (Multi Action Planning System) was developed by Marsha Forest and Judith Snow at McGill University. They developed MAPS as a process to be used when students with special needs moved from segregated special education classrooms to integrated neighborhood school classrooms. MAPS is a way of looking at the whole child in his or her whole life — classroom, school, home, and community. The process was designed to include parents as partners in their children's education. Although MAPS was initially developed for students with intellectual or multiple challenges, it is now used for any student for whom the school and home need to come together and agree on a plan.

After using the MAPS process, teachers began to see the incredible benefit of looking at students in this way, of receiving input from many people in a child's life, and in developing in-depth and consistent plans. Modifications of this process sprang up in many schools. Shorter and less in-depth sessions were used with students whose needs were less complex but who could benefit from consistent planning. In fact, many teachers have told us that they wish they had the time to use this process with all the students in their classroom.

The focused conversation of a MAPS session helps all participants become not just informed, but enabled to work more productively as a team with a student.

MAPS is a collaborative problem-solving process. The process relies on everyone's input in terms of who the student is and what he or she is able to do. Teachers, parents, and students, through participation in the process, tend to put aside any disagreements and focus on a mutually agreed-upon plan.

Focusing on One Student

1. Who will attend the meeting?

MAPS is a very open process; anyone who can add some information that would help make a meaningful and successful plan should come. The school personnel, along with the parents and student, decide who should attend. Each key person has a different relationship with the student, knows the student in a different way, and therefore will see the student differently. All key people will have different views on what works with this student. These divergent ideas are what makes the meeting rich and meaningful.

2. Who will facilitate?

It is best if the facilitator is an "outside person" in the sense that they may not know the student very well and have no personal agenda or preconceived ideas on what the outcomes of the meeting should be.

The facilitator does not participate in the content of the meeting. Instead, this person ensures that the meeting follows a process, that everyone has a chance to talk, that no one dominates, that ideas are recorded clearly and concisely, that the time frame is respected, and that a plan is made, or at least begun, by the end of the meeting. The facilitator needs to be adept at clarifying and clustering the ideas put forward, listening carefully and respectfully to each individual, and encouraging ideas from each person.

3. What needs to happen before the meeting?

Set a time: A meeting time that is agreeable to all needs to be determined. Usually these meetings occur after school or, if teachers can be released, they can be scheduled during the school day. In order to reach a plan, 1-1/2 hours is the *minimum* that should be scheduled.

Focus your thinking: Each invitee should receive a copy of the following questions to review.

> What are your dreams for _____ (the student)?
> What are your concerns/nightmares?
> What are his/her strengths?
> What are his/her needs?

If a person cannot attend, he or she might give input on paper to someone who will be present.

Sometimes the student is asked these questions:

> What are your dreams for yourself?

What are your concerns?
What are your strengths? or What are you really good at?
What are your needs? or What do you think you need to work on?

If the student cannot write responses him/herself, then someone who is detached from the answers that the student gives can scribe for him or her or assist in some way.

The questions are intended to stimulate thinking only, to provide a focus for the conversation. They do not need to be filled out or brought to the meeting. Answers are never collected. Individuals will share what they want to share during the meeting itself. In some cases the student or a parent decides that it's best if the student is not in attendance.

4. How should the meeting be set up?

Ideally, the meeting will take place in a warm, comfortable room where chairs can be gathered in a circle and where everyone can see each other.

The facilitator will need to make up four charts (one for each question), have felt pens available for recording, and find a place to put up each of the charts after they are completed so that the group can refer back to them.

5. How should the meeting unfold?

Begin with a welcome and a review of the objectives and roles. Next, gather and record information on the charts about dreams, concerns, strengths, and needs. Follow this discussion with a short break, then set priorities for planning based on the information gathered on the charts. Finally, begin to make a plan.

A Model MAPS Meeting

M Multi
A Action
P Planning
S System

Kevin is a Grade 5 student. Kevin's classroom teacher feels Kevin is being challenged by the work he is given in school, but Kevin's parents do not. They would like to see some changes in Kevin's program, and would like some input on how it's done. Kevin's teacher and the parents have met many times and have been unable to resolve the issue to the parents' satisfaction.

Step 1: Welcome/Objectives/Roles

Facilitator: I'd like to thank all of you for coming to spend some time talking about Kevin and his program here at school. Before we start the meeting, I want to be sure that everyone here knows who everyone else is. Let's take a minute to go around the table and have each person say their name and explain their relationship with Kevin.

Kevin, a friend of Kevin's, the classroom teacher, the parents, a resource teacher, the principal, and the facilitator introduce themselves.

Facilitator: Thank you. I'm Jesse, and I also work as a resource teacher in the school, but not with Kevin's classroom.

Today, we are going to be working together for about one and a half hours. During that time we will be using a planning process to look at Kevin's strengths and needs, what is currently happening for Kevin in school, and what everyone would like to see happen for Kevin. This process depends on everyone sharing their dreams and concerns for Kevin, and then looking at his strengths and needs. By the end of the meeting, we will begin to make a plan together.

Kevin, I want to encourage you to speak up as much as possible, even though it might be difficult to talk in front of everyone. It is really important for all of us to know what you think about each of the questions that I ask.

The facilitator explains his role is to ask the questions, record the information, and move the group toward a plan. He will seek to clarify the others' thinking.

Facilitator: We are going to work through the four questions I gave you to think about. Then we will have a short break, prioritize the areas we want to look at, and begin to make a plan.

Step 2: Gather and record information on the charts about dreams, concerns, strengths, and needs

Facilitator: We are going to begin by looking at dreams: the dreams you have for yourself, Kevin, and the dreams that your mom and dad, and your teachers, have for you. These dreams might be for this year in Grade 5. They may be for your high-school years or for you as an adult. Because we want to be sure we hear everyone's dreams for Kevin, we'll start by going around the circle. If you want to pass, just ask us to come back to you.

Kevin, would you feel comfortable starting? What is a dream you have for yourself?

Kevin: I'd like to become a paleontologist after I graduate.

The facilitator begins recording information on the appropriate chart, and continues to record all the information given throughout the meeting.

Facilitator: Really, you said two dreams there: one to become a paleontologist, and the other, to graduate. Is that right?

Kevin: Yes, I guess so.

Facilitator: Are you thinking you'd be a paleontologist after graduating from high school or university?

Kevin: Well, I was thinking high school, but I also think I'd like to go to university some day, too.

Facilitator: Okay. Thank you, Kevin. (to Kevin's mother) Ann, what is one of your dreams for Kevin?

Mother: I'd like to see Kevin challenged this year in school, and all through the rest of elementary and high school.

Facilitator: Are there any specific areas you're thinking about?

Mother: Mostly in math, but also in writing.

The facilitator next invites Kevin's teacher to speak.

Teacher: My dream for Kevin is that he graduates from university, has a successful career, and maintains the same attitude that he has now of caring for others and being willing to assist others who don't do as well as he does. Basically, that he continues to be such a kind and caring individual.

The facilitator summarizes these ideas as best she can.

Facilitator: Does that sum up what you were saying or was there more?

Teacher: No, that's fine.

The facilitator continues to gather and record information, often asking for clarification to be sure what is being recorded is really what the person is meaning. If only one area of the child's development is being talked about, the facilitator may probe. For example: "We have quite a few dreams for Kevin about his future in terms of education and his career. Does anyone have other dreams for Kevin, for example, about his emotional or social life, family, friends?"

After going around the circle two or three times and recording a wide range of ideas, the facilitator concludes the dreams area.

Facilitator: I see a lot of dreams here for you, Kevin. Do you have any others you'd like to add before we move on? Or does anyone else have another one?

The participants indicate that they are satisfied with the list.

Facilitator: We'll put the dream chart over here for now. If at any time during the meeting you'd like to add to it, please do so.

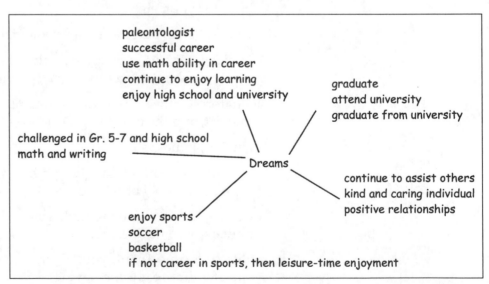

Facilitator: We're now going to look at any concerns we have for Kevin. These concerns may be things we are afraid might get in the way of his reaching the dreams that we've talked about. Again, Kevin, if you don't mind, we'll start with you.

Kevin: Well, I've thought about this one a lot since you gave me the questions. I couldn't really think of any concerns, but now that we've talked about my dreams, I guess I worry that my eyesight will get worse and I won't be able to get a good job or drive.

Facilitator: Thanks, Kevin. I can see that could really be a concern.

The facilitator begins recording information on concerns.

Facilitator: Ann, we'll move on to you.

Mother: I'm concerned that Kevin might lose interest in school if he's bored, and then won't complete school and go to university. I want so badly for him to stay motivated, be keen to try new things, and not feel he's just doing things over and over. I'm afraid if he has to do multiplication questions again he's just going to give up and say, "To heck with it, I'm bored."

Facilitator: So, there are a number of concerns there: one, that he'll be bored, then not complete high school and university; and two, that he'll give up. I also heard that you're concerned that he's repeating too many things at school, things that he already knows, such as multiplication. Is that right?

Mother: That is exactly right.

The facilitator turns to the classroom teacher.

Teacher: My concerns are similar to Ann's. I love to watch Kevin learn because he's keen, but I too am afraid that he might get discouraged. I guess my concern is that, because Kevin is such a nice guy, he won't tell me when he already knows something, when something is boring or redundant to him. I can't always know.

Facilitator: So you're concerned that Kevin will just continue to do something like multiplication even when he knows he doesn't need any more practice. Why?

Teacher: Oh, because he doesn't want to be a bother maybe. Or maybe he doesn't understand that teachers need to know that information, that most teachers, if approached politely, would be willing to listen to him.

Facilitator: Okay. Do my notes sum it up?

Teacher: Yes.

As with the dreams, the facilitator continues to go around the circle, clarifying and probing for information. After a wide range of ideas are gathered, the facilitator again brings this focus to a close.

Facilitator: There have been some concerns voiced about Kevin's academic program, his future, his eyesight, and his motivation and assertiveness to be sure he's challenged. Does anyone have any other concerns to express before we move on?

No one offers any more so this chart is put up beside the dreams.

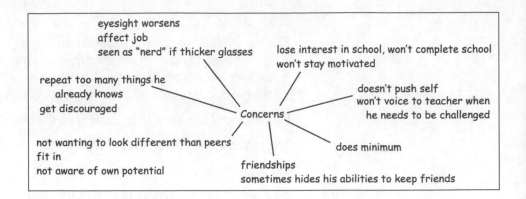

The strengths area is then addressed in a similar fashion, and then the needs area.

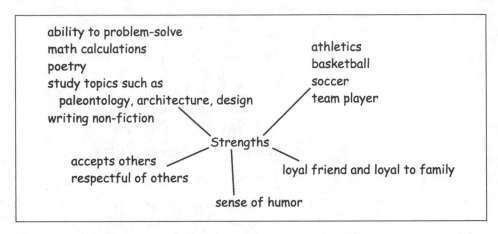

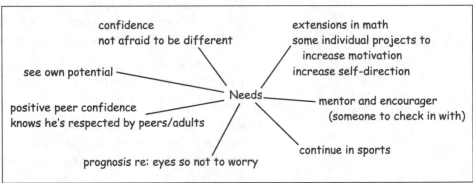

Facilitator: Before taking a short break, I'd like you to take a look at the four charts up on the wall. We have gathered a lot of information about Kevin, and I see some categories emerging: academic challenges, confidence, and medical. Do you see any others?

Father: I think those are the main ones.

Facilitator: Okay. If you see any other connections during the break, please let me know. Also, during the next ten minutes, think about priorities. Which of these areas do you think is the most important to address first?

Everyone takes a ten-minute break while the facilitator looks over the charts and formulates a plan for the next section.

Step 3: Set priorities for planning based on the information gathered on the charts

Facilitator: Are there any other areas that you thought of?

Mother: I think those three cover them.

Facilitator: Then let's look at what our priorities are for Kevin. Does anyone feel strongly about any one or two areas?

Teacher: The area of challenging Kevin in his academic work is the one that I think is the most important to tackle first. Kevin and his parents seem very concerned about that. I certainly want to do a good job in meeting Kevin's needs, and before we leave I'd love to be able to say we had at least the beginnings of a plan.

Facilitator: Do others of you think beginning on academics is the priority? Kevin, what do you think?

Kevin: Yes, I think that's the most important, though I'm interested in learning how to be more confident. Could we look at both?

Mother: I'd like to begin with challenging Kevin and then move to confidence. I also think the medical part is important and I'm wondering if that one could be dealt with by working with our family doctor.

Others nod in agreement. The facilitator writes the three areas on the chart paper called Plan.

Step 4: The group begins to make a plan

Facilitator: Okay, let's begin by developing a plan to ensure that Kevin's program is challenging. Then, if there's time, we'll move to confidence. In fact, these two areas may tie in nicely together. Your mom can deal with the medical aspects. Does that sound okay, Kevin?

Kevin: Yep.

Facilitator: Who would like to begin?

Resource teacher: It looks like the two subject areas that Kevin and his parents and teacher are concerned about are math and language arts. As far as math goes, we could give Kevin the chapter tests and, if he achieves the learning outcomes, he could skip the practice on those. We could use both the Grade 5 and 6 texts and supplemental materials, if everyone is agreeable to acceleration in math.

Teacher: I'm fine about acceleration in math. Kevin could use the Grade 5–7 concepts and learning outcomes and achieve them all this year and next if he can. We could easily use the learning outcomes and, when he achieves them, he could move on. There are a few challenges though. The texts don't cover all of the learning outcomes, especially problem-solving, reflection, and the use of mathematical language. He would miss the learning that comes from group interactions in math. And since we do not use all the chapters in the text, we would

Plan for Kevin

Re: Math
☐ Do work in class.
☐ Same topic areas as class is working on, but with extended materials (from Grades 6 and 7).
☐ Talk with Grades 6 and 7 teachers.
☐ Keep records of all areas completed.

Re: Language Arts Research
☐ Librarian will be mentor.
☐ Do research assignments (projects) with a small group of students in classroom (possibly three other students).
☐ Work about three times a week on project. Some individual time on weekends, evenings.
☐ Parents will be involved in supporting/encouraging/ extending individual work (public library, linking with experts in the community.

have to look carefully at the materials and the areas he'd be missing in the curriculum. Maybe I could meet with Grade 6 and 7 teachers to map out a plan. What do you think of that, Kevin?

Kevin: Well, I'd like to do harder math, but does that mean I'd have to leave the room to do math with the other grades?

Facilitator: Does that concern you?

Kevin: Yeah. I don't want to leave. I don't mind doing other work, but I don't want to make a big deal out of it.

Facilitator: What are you saying? That you don't want the other kids to notice, that you're uncomfortable going to other classes, or what?

Kevin: Well, I'm not sure. I guess I like being in my own class and I like doing math with my friends. I do like the idea of doing harder math 'cause I know I can do it, but I don't really want to sit there doing it all on my own.

Facilitator: So, if we can figure out a way to give you more difficult math concepts or applications in your own classroom, perhaps on the same topic that everyone else is doing or something similar, would that suit you?

Kevin: Yes.

Teacher: Well, maybe with extension materials, Kevin could first do all the chapters that are similar to the ones we're doing. For example, we're working on geometry now, so if Kevin achieves the Grade 5 geometry learning outcomes, then he could pull out alternative tasks and use parallel, but more challenging, geometry learning outcomes. At the end of the year he will have acquired some of the concepts and learning outcomes normally taught in Grades 6 and 7.

Principal: As long as we talk with the Grade 6 and 7 teachers about this, that might be okay. However, we'd need to keep a record of exactly what has been completed. I'm wondering if there are parts of the curriculum that are already challenging enough for Kevin or that would need only slight adaptation.

Dad: All this is okay, as long as we are talking about a plan for Grades 5, 6, and 7 and not just from now until the end of June. Everyone would have to agree because, if Kevin has to repeat outcomes in the same Grade 6 textbook next year, he will be more bored than ever.

Resource teacher: You're right. We'll need to talk with the teacher next year in September, but I doubt there would be a problem, as we have several other students in the upper grades on accelerated programs.

The discussion continues and a plan is made for math and language arts with Kevin having to take more personal responsibility for speaking up and letting the classroom teacher and his parents know how things are going.

Step 5: Set up a follow-up meeting

A one-hour follow-up meeting is scheduled for one month away, to discuss confidence and medical concerns, and to get an update on how the math and research projects are going.

Reflections on MAPS

These planning sessions are time-consuming, but generally very rewarding. Many teachers leave wishing there was time to have meetings like this for more students. Parents feel heard and students benefit by having a program more closely designed for them. Since all of the major players are in attendance, more support and understanding between home and school can be generated.

These planning meetings can also be used to look at such issues as school-wide behavior, inclusion, clubs and teams. Furthermore, staffs, classrooms, student councils, and parent advisory groups can use the process to help set goals and plan or determine staff development needs. The MAPS session is a process that respects and includes all those involved, helping a group of individuals work together to address concerns, make a plan, and take action.

Appendix 1: People Search Strategy

Adapted from Bellanca and Fogarty (1986), *Catch Them Thinking*.

People Search is a great strategy to get students talking and sharing their knowledge with each other. It is also a good way to review material before a text, or find out how much students know on a new topic of study. It promotes active listening and develops skills in clarification and paraphrasing.

1. Create a page with four to six boxes on it. At the top write the words "Find someone who..." and write ideas in the boxes. For example, "... can *describe* what it feels like to be included"; "...can *tell* you about a time they helped someone"; "...can *imagine* what it would be like if everyone felt they belonged"; "...can *explain* why our school has a code of conduct"; "...can *list* four things they did this week to make someone else feel good"; "...can *name* at least one person in the school they can go to for help. (Note the words in italics that help to promote different kinds of critical thinking skills — be sure that all the students will be able to answer at least one or two of the questions.)

2. Explain to the students what a people search is all about. Show them the sheet and tell them that they will be moving around the classroom finding different individuals who can answer each question. (They must have a different person for each question.)

   - Tell the students that the people they talk to must be able to explain the answer in such a way that they are able to retell it (active listening).
   - Direct them to write down the answer or key words, or an illustration to help them remember the answer given. They should say the answer back to the person and have them sign their sheets when they are sure they understand.

3. Instruct the students to circulate and ask if they can help other students once their sheets are filled in.

4. When all of the students have completed their sheets, meet as a group and debrief the answers. You might want to make a master sheet and record some of the variety of answers.

Appendix 2: Think of a Time Strategy

Used with permission of the authors Brownlie, Close, and Wingren, *Tomorrow's Classroom Today.*

1. Students are grouped in threes.

2. Students are instructed to "think of a time when..." around a topic, and share their thinking with their small group. For example, the topic could be inclusion, bullying, helping out, achieving beyond your expectations, etc.

3. The first "think of a time" is as a participant — when something happens to you or you were the actor. "Think of a time when someone helped you be included."

4. After small-group exchange and class sharing, one student per group moves to join new group.

5. The second "think of a time" is as a witness — when you saw something. "Think of a time when you watched someone reach out and include another."

6. After small-group exchange and class sharing, the second student from each group moves to find a new group.

7. The third "think of a time" is as a causal agent — when you planned or caused something to happen. "Think of a time when you reached out and helped someone be included."

8. After exchanging views in the small group and with the whole class, students return to their original triad.

9. The teacher helps isolate the critical learning variables that have been shared.

10. Students reflect on the process in their triads.

11. Students reflect personally.

Appendix 3: Forms for Curriculum Adaptations

See pages 141 and 142.

PROGRAM ANALYSIS WORKSHEET
©Cranston/Meston, Maple Ridge

Name: _____
Curricular Area: _____

Date Initiated: _____
Review Date: _____

Class Learning Outcomes • highlight appropriate objectives	Evaluation	As is	IS IT APPROPRIATE? with adapted goals/expectations, presentation, evaluation, materials, assistance, or environment	Person Responsible	Individual Learning Outcomes (materials, criteria, review date)	Evaluation Comments (date achieved)

Pembroke Publishers © 2011 *Learning in Safe Schools, revised edition* by Faye Brownlie and Judith King ISBN 978-1-55138-266-1

CRITICAL ACTIVITIES MATRIX
© Ives/Meston, Maple Ridge

Name: _____

Date: _____

Review Date: _____

CLASSROOM ACTIVITIES

INDIVIDUAL LEARNING OUTCOMES

Pembroke Publishers © 2011 *Learning in Safe Schools, revised edition* by Faye Brownlie and Judith King ISBN 978-1-55138-266-1

Annotated Bibliography of Classroom Resources

Picture Books (Kindergarten to Grade 7)

Blos, Joan. (Stephen Gammell, illus.) *Old Henry*. New York, NY: Morrow, 1990. Henry gets tired of his neighbors bothering him about his beat-up old house. So he moves away. Now neither he nor the neighbors are happy.

THEMES: exclusion, accepting differences

Browne, Anthony. *Little Beauty*. Cambridge, MA: Candlewick Press, 2008. A unique friendship develops between a gorilla and a cat.

THEMES: friendship, empathy

Campbell, Nicola I. *Sin-chi's Canoe*. Toronto, ON: Groundwood Books, 2008. Shi-shi-etko and her brother attend a residential school. He finds solace in the canoe given to him by his sister.

THEMES: family, resilience, surviving

Cannon, Janell. *Stellaluna*. New York, NY: Harcourt Brace, 1999. A young fruit bat, separated from her mother, falls into a nest of birds. Stellaluna tries to adjust to eating bugs, sleeping at night, and not hanging by her feet. She and her three bird friends learn to appreciate each other for their similarities and their differences.

_____. *Trupp: A Fuzzhead Tale*. New York, NY: Harcourt Brace, 1998. A fuzzhead animal leaves his home to explore the world, finding out about friendship and danger.

THEMES: journey, belonging

Fleming, Virginia. (Floyd Cooper, illus.) *Be Good to Eddie Lee*. New York, NY: Putnam and Grosset Group, 1993. When a young girl gets to know a boy with a disability, she discovers that what matters is not how you look, but what's in your heart.

THEMES: exclusion, friendship, diversity

Gregory, Nan. (Ron Lightburn, illus.) *How Smudge Came*. Red Deer, AB: Red Deer College Press, 1997. When her group home won't allow her to keep a puppy she finds, Cindy feels very alone. Then she finds she has friends after all.

THEMES: exclusion/inclusion, empathy, belonging

Madden, Don. *The Wartville Wizard*. New York, NY: Aladdin Paperbacks, 1986. An old man gets tired of cleaning up everyone else's garbage. Then strange things begin to happen!

THEME: caring for our world

Muir, Stephen. (Mary Jane Muir, illus.) *Albert's Old Shoes*. Toronto, ON: Stoddart, 1996. Albert gets so frustrated about everyone teasing him about his beat-up shoes that one day, in total frustration, he kicks a soccer ball an amazing distance. All of the children are wildly impressed.

THEMES: exclusion, belonging, peer pressure

Polacco, Patricia. *Babushka Baba Yaga*. New York, NY: Putnam Publishing Group, 1993. Baba Yaga yearns to hold and care for a baby the way other older women enjoy their grandchildren. When she disguises herself as a visiting babushka, she is soon loved by a little boy. Then rumors poison her happiness.

THEMES: exclusion, belonging, rumors, not judging others

_____. *The Keeping Quilt*. New York, NY: Simon and Schuster Children's Books, 1988. A very special quilt, made from garments that have come from Russia, is passed down from generation to generation. This book looks at traditions that belong to groups of people and how things both change and stay the same over time.

THEMES: belonging, journeys, love, family

_____. *Mrs. Katz and Tush*. New York, NY: Bantam Little Rooster Book, 1992. Love grows between an old woman, a young boy, and a cat.

THEMES: belonging, love, friendship

_____. *Thank You, Mr. Falker*. New York, NY: Putnam Publishing Group, 1998. A young girl who has difficulty learning to read feels the stigma of being "different." Finally she meets a teacher who makes a big difference to her life.

THEMES: belonging, acceptance of self, learning journey

_____. *The Trees of the Dancing Goats*. New York, NY: Simon and Schuster Children's Books, 1996. During a time of sickness in a small community, a Jewish family helps their neighbors celebrate Christmas.

THEMES: friendship, inclusion, giving

Rylant, Cynthia. (Stephen Gammell, illus.) *The Relatives Came*. New York, NY: Bradbury Press, 1985. Relatives travel to visit, stay, help and love each other.

THEMES: caring, inclusion, belonging

Van Allsburg, Chris. *Just a Dream*. New York, NY: Houghton Mifflin, 1990. A boy dreams of what will happen to the world if we do not take care of it.

THEMES: care for the world, personal journey to understanding

Tan, Shaun. *The Arrival*. New York, NY: Scholastic, 2006. A wordless picture book depicting the struggles and joys of immigrating to a new country.

THEMES: journey, belonging

Watt, Melanie. *Scaredy Squirrel*. Toronto, ON: Kids Can Press, 2006. Scaredy Squirrel is afraid of everything, including flying, which is especially a concern given that he is a flying squirrel. He learns to conquer his fear.

THEMES: overcoming fear, personal journey

Wild, Margaret. (Julie Vivas, illus.) *The Very Best of Friends*. San Diego, CA: Harcourt Brace, 1989. When Jessie's husband, James, dies, Jessie becomes depressed and ignores his favorite pet, William. One day Jessie looks at William and is startled to see that he has become mean and lean. She begins to make amends and works toward becoming the very best of friends.

THEMES: belonging, exclusion

Williams, Margery. *The Velveteen Rabbit*. Philadelphia, PA: Running Press, 1981. If you belong, you become real. It does not matter what you look like; it's how you are treated that makes you real, makes you belong.

THEMES: belonging

Primary Books

Aliki. *Feelings*. New York, NY: Morrow, 1986.

THEME: belonging

Bourgeois, Paulette. (Brenda Clark, illus.) *Franklin Goes to School*. Toronto, ON: Kids Can Press, 1995.

THEMES: acceptance of self, learning journey

_____. *Franklin in the Dark*. Toronto, ON: Kids Can Press, 1997.

_____. *Franklin Plays the Game*. Toronto, ON: Kids Can Press, 1995. Franklin discovers he needs practice and encouragement in order to improve.

_____. *Franklin Rides a Bike*. Toronto, ON: Kids Can Press, 1997. Franklin learns that some things are harder for some people than others, but that he can ride a bike if he keeps practicing.

THEME: learning journey

_____. *Franklin's Secret Club*. Toronto, ON: Kids Can Press, 1998.

THEMES: exclusion, belonging

Bunting, Eve. (Donald Carrick, illus.) *The Wednesday Surprise*. New York, NY: Houghton Mifflin, 1990. A little girl teaches her grandmother to read.

THEMES: love, learning journey, sharing

Elliott, Laura Malone. *Hunter's Best Friend at School*. New York, NY: HarperCollins Publishers, 2002. Hunter begins kindergarten with his best friend, Stripe, who unfortunately keeps getting him into trouble.

THEMES: friendship, belonging, choosing the right path

Fitch, Sheree. (Darcia Labrosse, illus.) *If You Could Wear My Sneakers: A Book about Children's Rights*. Toronto, ON: Doubleday, 1997. The author has created poems to help children understand the United Nations Rights of the Child.

THEMES: safety, belonging, acceptance

Fox, Mem. (Pamela Lofts, illus.) *Koala Lou*. New York, NY: Harcourt Brace Jovanovich, 1988. A young Koala wonders about her busy mother's love and strives to win it back.

THEMES: unconditional love and acceptance, belonging

Gliori, Debi. *The Snow Lambs*. New York, NY: Scholastic, 1996. A young boy worries when his dog does not return in a snowstorm. The illustrations depict the separate journeys of the dog and the boy on the same pages.

THEMES: caring, belonging, journey

Helakoski, Leslie. *Woolbur*. New York, NY: HarperCollins Children's Books, 2008. Woolbur is a sheep who sets and follows his own course, much to his parents' distraction.

THEMES: belonging, differences, family

Henkes, Kevin. *Wemberly Worried*. New York, NY: Greenwillow Books, 2000. Wemberly heads off to Kindergarten, terribly worried that she will have no friends and not fit in.

THEMES: belonging, friendship

_____. *Chester's Way*. New York, NY: Morrow, 1997. Chester learns that he can be friends with kids and learn from them whether they are like him or not.

THEMES: friendship, individual differences, inclusion

_____. *Lilly's Purple Plastic Purse*. New York, NY: Greenwillow Books, 1996. This wonderful book is full of emotion, Lilly's feelings, and her ways of expressing them. Lilly learns a lot about herself and her teacher on a journey of the heart.

THEMES: belonging, feelings, journey

Hills, Tad. *Duck & Goose*. New York, NY: Schwartz & Wade Books, 2006. Duck and Goose discover a soccer ball and each claim it as their own, mistakenly believing it to be an egg.

THEMES: friendship, solving problems

Joly, Fanny. *Mr. Fine, Porcupine*. San Francisco, CA: Chronicle Books, 1997.

THEME: friendship

Joose, Barbara. (Barbara Lavalle, illus.) *Mama, Do You Love Me?* San Francisco, CA: Chronicle Books, 1991. An Inuit mother reassures her daughter that though she may feel many emotions, she will still love her "forever and always."

THEMES: unconditional love, belonging

Kraus, Robert. (Jose Aruego, illus.) *Leo the Late Bloomer*. New York, NY: HarperCollins Children's Books, 1998. Leo, a little tiger, has difficulty learning to read, write, talk, eat, and draw, but given the gift of time he learns and blooms.

THEME: learning journey

LeBox, Annette. (Heather Holbrook, illus.) *Miss Rafferty's Rainbow Socks*. Toronto, ON: HarperCollins, 1996. A friendship between an older woman and a young girl is portrayed in a magical way. Each of them gives up their most prized possession for the other.

THEMES: friendship, belonging, giving

Lester, Helen. (Lynn Munsinger, illus.) *A Porcupine Named Fluffy*. Boston, MA: Houghton Mifflin, 1989. Fluffy is not fluffy no matter how hard he tries. He ventures out into the world and finds out that it is okay to be himself and even to laugh at himself.

THEME: acceptance of self

_____. *Tacky the Penguin*. Boston, MA: Houghton Mifflin, 1988.

THEMES: diversity, belonging

_____. *Three Cheers for Tacky*. Boston, MA: Houghton Mifflin, 1996. Tacky tries hard to be like the other penguins, but it is his uniqueness that saves the day!

THEMES: diversity, belonging

Lionni, Leo. *Swimmy*. New York, NY: Random House, 1973. With Swimmy to help them, smaller fish form a shape that looks like one large fish and frighten their enemies away.

THEMES: belonging, working together

Lunn, Janet. (Kim LaFave, illus.) *Amos's Sweater*. Toronto, ON: Groundwood, 1988. Amos is an old, cold sheep who is tired of giving up his wool. Aunt Hattie and Uncle Henry come to understand his point of view.

THEME: belonging

McBratney, Sam. (Anita Jeram, illus.) *Guess How Much I Love You*. Cambridge, MA: Candlewick Press, 1994.

THEMES: love, belonging

Munsch, Robert. (Eugenie Fernandes, illus.) *Ribbon Rescue*. Toronto, ON: Scholastic Canada, 1999. Jillian gives away all of the ribbons from her traditional Mohawk dress to help others.

THEMES: belonging, giving

O'Neill, Alexis & Laura Huliska-Beith. *The Recess Queen*. New York, NY: Scholastic, 2002. The playground is ruled and bullied by Mean Jean until a new student arrives, a small girl who doesn't know the rules.

THEMES: belonging, bullying, inclusion

Plantos, Ted. (Heather Collins, illus.) *Heather Hits Her First Home Run*. Windsor, ON: Black Moss Press, 1989. Heather learns the value of perseverance.

THEMES: friendship, practice, and team spirit

Raschka, Christopher. *Yo! Yes?* New York, NY: Orchard Books, 1993.

THEME: friendship

Rath, Tom & Mary Reckmeyer. *How Full Is Your Bucket? For kids*. New York, NY: Gallup Press, 2009. Felix has a bucket that he either empties or fills each day as he interacts with others. He learns how easy it is to fill others' buckets.

THEMES: inclusion, making a difference, empathy

Rylant, Cynthia. (Arthur Howard, illus.) *Mr. Putter and Tabby Pour the Tea*. San Diego, CA: Harcourt Brace, 1994. Mr. Putter goes to the animal shelter to find a cat like him — old with thinning hair and creaking bones.

THEME: friendship

Simmie, Lois. (Cynthia Nugent, illus.) *Mister Got to Go: The Cat That Wouldn't Leave*. Red Deer, AB: Red Deer College Press, 1995. A stray cat becomes part of a hotel family.

THEME: belonging

Wild, Margaret. (Julie Vivas, illus.) *Our Granny*. New York, NY: Ticknor and Fields, 1994.

THEMES: respecting diversity, belonging

Yorinks, Arthur. (Mort Drucker, illus.) *Whitefish Will Rides Again!* New York, NY: HarperCollins Children's Books, 1994.

THEME: non-violent conflict resolution

Intermediate/Middle Books

Abbott, Tony. *Firegirl*. New York, NY: Little, Brown and Co., 2006. Into Tom's seventh grade class comes a new student, Jessica. Jessica has been severely burned and evokes fear in the other students.

THEMES: understanding differences, courage

Boraks-Nemetz, Lillian. *The Old Brown Suitcase*. Brentwood Bay, BC: Ben-Simon Publications, 1994. Having survived the Second World War in Poland, a fourteen-year-old girl now living in Canada struggles with English, memories, new ways and customs.

THEMES: belonging, identity

Collins, Suzanne. *The Hunger Games*. New York, NY: Scholastic, 2008. This futuristic novel sets 12- to 18-year olds against one another in a televised fight to the death.

THEMES: relationships, courage, family values

Ellis, Deborah. *Off to War: Voices of Soldiers' Children*. Toronto, ON: Groundwood Books, 2008. Ellis interviews children of Canadian and American soldiers who have been serving in Afghanistan and Iraq. They describe the impact of this absence on their lives.

THEMES: journey, family, courage

Filipovic, Zlata. *Zlata's Diary: A Child's Life in Sarajevo*. New York, NY: Viking Penguin, 1995. A young teenager struggles to make sense of life in war-torn Sarajevo in her diary. This true story was originally published by UNICEF.

THEMES: belonging, identity

Garrigue, Sheila. *The Eternal Spring of Mr. Ito*. New York, NY: Simon and Schuster Children's Books, 1994. Evacuated from war-torn England during the Second World War, Sara is living with relatives in Vancouver when the internment of Japanese begins. She tries to make sense of events.

THEMES: diversity, courage

Gleitzman, Morris. *Sticky Beak*. New York, NY: Harcourt Brace Jovanovich, 1995. Rowena, who is mute, worries that the baby her father and new mother are expecting will be loved more than she is.

THEMES: belonging, family, change

Golenbock, Peter. (Paul Bacon, illus.) *Teammates*. New York, NY: Harcourt Brace Jovanovich, 1990. This picture book talks about discrimination against blacks in America, focusing on the true story of Jackie Robinson, the first black player in major-league baseball.

THEMES: exclusion, courage

Jordan-Fenton, Christy & Margaret Pokiak-Fenton. *Fatty Legs*. Vancouver, BC: Annick Press, 2010. This is Margaret's true story of leaving the High Arctic (because she wanted to learn to read) and going to residential school in Aklavik.

THEMES: family, belonging, courage

Kidd, Diana. *Onion Tears*. New York, NY: Orchard Books, 1991. A Vietnamese immigrant to Australia suffers so much rejection that she becomes mute.

THEMES: courage, belonging

Laird, Elizabeth. *Lost Riders*. London, UK: Macmillan Children's Books, 2008. Historical fiction. Until 2005, 3000 young boys from Pakistan and surrounding countries were working on camel farms and racing camels in the United Arab Emirates. This is their story.

THEMES: child exploitation, courage

Little, Jean. *From Anna*. New York, NY: HarperCollins Children's Books, 1973. Anna suffers much teasing about her clumsiness, but after her family immigrates to a new land, her visual impairment is discovered. See also *Listen for the Singing*, which continues Anna's adventures.

THEMES: belonging, journey

Lowry, Lois. *Number the Stars*. Boston, MA: Houghton Mifflin, 1995. Told from a Jewish girl's point of view, this story relates how the Danes saved many Jews around the time of the Second World War.

THEMES: courage, friendship

Matas, Carol. *Daniel's Story*. Richmond Hill, ON: Scholastic Canada, 1993. Daniel tells the story of his journey as a Jew from Frankfurt to Lodz to Auschwitz to Buchenwald.

THEME: journey

Matthews, L.S. *Fish*. New York, NY: Random House, 2004. In an unidentified war-torn country, the violence moves too close and a family of three plus a guide must cross the mountains and cross the border. They are accompanied by the protagonist's newly rescued fish.

THEMES: journey, relationships, hope

Paterson, Katherine. *The Great Gilly Hopkins*. New York, NY: HarperCollins Children's Books, 1987. A bright obstreperous child in a loving foster home comes to understand love and family too late to stay where she is. She eventually goes to her grandmother's and learns where her "true grit" comes from.

THEMES: belonging, journey

Sadiq, Nazneen. *Camels Can Make You Homesick and Other Stories*. Toronto, ON: James Lorimer, 1985. Five short stories of how new Canadians adjust to life in Canada.

THEMES: belonging, journey

Shyer, Marlene F. *Welcome Home, Jellybean*. New York, NY: Simon and Schuster Children's Books, 1988. Neil's sister comes home from an institution, changing his life and the lives of his parents.

THEMES: belonging, caring

Smucker, Barbara. *Jacob's Little Giant*. Markham, ON: Penguin, 1987. A young boy, tired of being the "baby," grows through caring for a flock of Canada geese.

THEME: journey

Voigt, Cynthia. *Homecoming*. New York, NY: Fawcett, 1987. Four children, abandoned by their mother, learn to care for each other and stick together at all costs.

THEMES: belonging, journey

Walters, Eric. *We All Fall Down*. Toronto, ON: Random House (Seal Books), 2006. Will is a ninth-grade student who joins his father to shadow him at his workplace in the Twin Towers on September 11, 2001.

THEMES: courage, family, belonging

Wilson, Budge. *A House Far from Home*. Richmond Hill, ON: Scholastic Canada, 1986.

THEMES: belonging, accepting diversity

————. *Oliver's Wars*. Toronto, ON: Stoddart, 1992. While his father serves in Saudi Arabia during the Gulf War, Oliver and his twin brother live with grandparents in Halifax. They deal with matters of safety, fear, a new school, and fitting in.

THEMES: belonging, courage

Yee, Paul. *The Bone Collector's Son*. Vancouver, BC: Tradewind Books, 2003. Bing-wing Chan is a 14-year-old second-generation Chinese boy living in Vancouver. He is called in to help his father with his job as a bone collector. Initially resentful, he comes to terms with his Canadian and Chinese background.

THEMES: family, belonging, journey

Music

Humphries, Pat. *Common Thread*. Wood Lake Books. Sheet Music.

THEME: belonging, community

Lea, Judy. *Too Much Work to Do*. Vancouver, BC: Tyrannosockus Productions, 1997. Compact Disk/Tape. Songs: "If You Care," "Every Little Thing," "If You Help Me"

THEME: belonging

Music for Little People. *Peace Is the World Smiling: A Peace Anthology for Families*. Redway, CA. Compact Disk. Songs: "Peace Is the World Smiling," "Hug the Earth," "Everybody Is Somebody," "Kids' Peace Song"

THEME: belonging, community

Raffi. *Bananaphone*. Vancouver, BC: Troubador Records, 1994. Compact Disk/Tape.

THEMES: care for the world, belonging

Rankin Family. *North Country*. EMI Music Canada. Compact Disk/Tape. Song: "We Will Rise Again"

THEME: community

Scott, Rick. *Philharmonic Fool*. Vancouver, BC: Jester Records, 1995. Compact Disk/Tape. Songs: "Grandma," "Angels Do," "You Make Me Happy"

THEMES: appreciating others, friendship

Thomas, Marlo, and Friends. *Free to Be You and Me*. Arista Records, 1983. Compact Disk/Tape.

THEMES: acceptance of self and others

Professional Bibliography

Allington, R., *What really matters for struggling readers (2nd ed)*. Boston, MA: Pearson, 2006.

Allington, Richard L., and Sean A. Walmsley (ed.). *No Quick Fix: Rethinking Literacy Programs in America's Elementary Schools*. Newark, DE: IRA, 1995.

Armstrong, Thomas. *Awakening Genius in the Classroom*. Alexandria, VA: ASCD, 1998.

Bellanca, J. *A guide to graphic organizers (2nd ed)*. Thousand Oaks, CA: Corwin Press, 2007.

Bendtro, Larry, Martin Brokenleg, and Steve Van Bockern. *Reclaiming Youth at Risk: Our Hope for the Future*. Bloomington, IN: Solution Tree Press, 1990.

Bennett, B., & P. Smilanich. *Classroom management: A thinking and caring approach*. Toronto, ON: Bookation Inc. 1994.

Black, Paul, Christine Harrison, Clare Lee, Bethan Marshall, & Dylan Wiliam. *Assessment for Learning: Putting it into Practice*. Berkshire, UK: Open University Press, 2003.

Blankstein, Alan. *Failure is Not an Option: Six Principles that Guide Student Achievement in High-performing Schools*. Thousand Oaks, CA: Corwin Press, 2004.

Brownlie, F., C. Fullerton & L. Schnellert. *It's all about thinking: Collaborating to support all learners in mathematics and science*. Winnipeg, MB: Portage & Main Press, 2011.

Brownlie, F. & L. Schnellert. *It's all about thinking: Collaborating to support all learners in English, Social Studies, and Humanities*. Winnipeg, MB: Portage & Main Press, 2009.

Brownlie, F., C. Feniak & L. Schnellert. *Student Diversity: Classroom strategies to meet the learning needs of all students (2nd Ed)*. Markham, ON: Pembroke, 2006.

Brownlie, F. *Grand Conversations, Thoughtful Responses: A unique approach to literature circles*. Winnipeg, MB: Portage & Main Press, 2005.

Brownlie, Faye. *Literacy in the Middle Years*. http://insinc.com/ministry ofeducation/20041007/archive. html

Cameron, Caren, Betty Tate, Daphne MacNaughton, and Colleen Politano. *Recognition without Rewards*. Winnipeg, MB: Peguis, 1997.

Cunningham, Patricia M., and Richard L. Allington. *Classrooms That Work: They Can All Read & Write*. Reading, MA: Addison-Wesley, 1998.

DeBoer, Anita. *The Art of Consulting*. Chicago, IL: Arcturus Books, 1986.

_____. *Working Together: The Art of Consulting and Communicating*. Longmont, CO: Sopris West, 1995.

Elias, Maurice, et al. *Promoting Social and Emotional Learning: Guidelines for Educators*. Baltimore, MD: ASCD, 1997.

Eyre, R., and L. Eyre. *Teaching Your Children Values*. New York, NY: Simon and Schuster, 1993.

Fink, R. *Why Jane and John couldn't read – and how they learned: A new look at striving readers*. Newark, DE: IRA, 2006.

Fogarty, R. *Literacy matters: Strategies every teacher can use (2nd ed)*. Thousand Oaks, CA: Corwin Press, 2007.

Gibbs, J. *Tribes: A new way of learning together*. Santa Rosa, CA: Center Source, 1994.

Goleman, Daniel. *Emotional Intelligence*. New York, NY: Bantam, 1995.

Gossen, Diane. *It's All About We: Rethinking Discipline Using Restitution*. Saskatoon, SK: Chelsom Consulting Ltd., 2004.

Gossen, Diane and Judy Anderson. *Creating the Conditions: Leadership for Quality Schools*. Chapel Hill, NC: New View, 1995.

Gregory, Kathleen, Caren Cameron, and Anne Davis. *Setting and Using Criteria*. Boothbay, ME: Connections, 1997.

Harvey, S & A. Goudvis. *Strategies that work: Teaching comprehension for understanding and engagement*. Markham, ON: Pembroke, 2007.

Hattie, J. & H. Timperley. "The power of feedback." *Review of Educational Research*, 77 (1): 81–112.

Hingsburger, David. *Eye Opener*. Vancouver, BC: Family Support Institute Press, 1993.

Houston, Paul, Alan Blankstein, & Robert Cole. *Out of the Box Leadership*. Thousand Oaks, CA: Corwin Press, 2007.

Keefe, Charlotte Hendrick. *Label-Free Learning: Supporting Learners with Disabilities*. Portland, ME: Stenhouse, 1996.

Kidder, Rushworth. *Moral Courage*. New York, NY: HarperCollins, 2006.

Jensen, Eric. *Teaching with the Brain in Mind*. Baltimore, MD: ASCD, 1998.

Knox, Gerald. *Vegetables, Herbs and Fruit*. Des Moines, IA: Better Homes and Gardens, 1988.

Lang, Greg, and Chris Berberich. *All Children Are Special: Creating an Inclusive Classroom*. Portland, ME: Stenhouse, 1995.

Leach, Penelope. *Children First: What Society Must Do — and Is Not Doing — for Children Today*. London, UK: Vintage Books, 1994.

Maslow, A. H. *Toward a Psychology of Being (3rd ed)*. New York, NY: Wiley, 1998.

McGinnis, Ellen, and Arnold P. Goldstein. *Skillstreaming in Early Childhood: Teaching Prosocial Skills to the Preschool and Kindergarten Child*. Champaign, IL: Research Press, 1990.

_____. *Skillstreaming the Elementary School Child: New Strategies and Perspectives for Teaching Prosocial Skills* (rev. ed.). Champaign, IL: Research Press, 1997.

Perske, Robert. *Circle of Friends*. Burlington, ON: Welch, 1988.

Pink, Daniel. *Drive: The Surprising Truth About What Motivates Us*. New York, NY: Riverhead Books, 2009.

Robinson, Ken. *Out of Our Minds: Learning to be Creative*. West Sussex, UK: Capstone, 2001.

Robinson, Ken. *The Element: How Finding Your Passion Changes Everything*. New York, NY: Penguin, 2009.

Rose, David H. & Anne Meyer. *Teaching Every Student in the Digital Age: Universal Design for Learning*. Alexandria, VA: ASCD, 2002.

Rosencrans, G. *The Spelling Book: Teaching children how to spell, not what to spell*. Newark, DE: IRA, 1998.

Roller, Cathy M. *So...What's a Tutor to Do?* Newark, DE: IRA, 1998.

Santa, Carol Minnick. *Project CRISS*. Dubuque, IA: Kendall/Hunt, 1996.

Schonert-Reichl, Kim.
http://bctf.ca/uploadedFiles/News_and_events/Public_Ed_Conference/Every_kid_counts/Schonert-ReichlPresentation.pdf http://www.educ.ubc.ca/research/ksr/docs/ uw-middlechildhood_summary.pdf (2008)

Sheridan, Susan Rich. *Brain Compatible Teaching and Learning (Course syllabus)*. http://drawingwriting.com/syllabus.pdf

Silver, H., R. Strong, and M. Perini. *The Strategic Teacher*. Alexandria, VA: ASCD, 2007.

Stainback, S., and W. Stainback (ed.). *Support Networks for Inclusive Schooling*. Baltimore, MD: Paul H. Brookes Publishing, 1990.

Tovani, C. *I read it, but I don't get it: Comprehension strategies for adolescent learners*. Portland, ME: Stenhouse, 2000.

_____. *Do I really have to teach reading? Content comprehension, Grades 6–12*. Portland, ME: Stenhouse, 2004.

Thousand, J, R. Villa, & A. Nevin. *Differentiating Instruction: Collaborative Planning and Teaching for Universally Designed Learning*. Thousand Oaks, CA: Corwin Press, 2007.

Villa, R., and J. Thousand. *Creating an Inclusive School*. Baltimore, MD: ASCD, 1995.

Wells, J., & J. Reid. *Writing Anchors*. Markham, ON: Pembroke, 2004.

Wheatley, J. *Strategic Spelling: Moving beyond word memorization in the middle grades*. Newark, DE: IRA, 2005.

Index